The Filet Crochet Book

For instructions see page 64

Published in 1990 by Sterling Publishing Co., Inc.
387 Park Avenue South, New York, NY 10016.

Copyright © 1990 Altamont Press.

A Sterling / Lark Book
Produced by Altamont Press, Inc.
50 College Street, Asheville, NC 28801

ISBN 0-8069-5822-7

Translations: Networks, Inc.
Art Director: Rob Pulleyn
Production: Judy Clark
Editor: Dawn Cusick
Typesetting: Diana Deakin
Valuable Assistance: Nola Theiss

Library of Congress
Cataloging-in-Publication Data
Rankin, Chris.
        The filet crochet book / by Chris Rankin;
        with an introduction by Nola Theiss.
                p.   cm.
        "A Sterling / Lark book."
        ISBN 0-8069-5822-7
        1. Crocheting—Patterns.   I. Title.
        TT820.R336   1989
        746.43'4--dc20   89-21904
                                        CIP

Photos on the following pages © Verlags Gruppe
Bauer, Hamburg, Germany: 1, 4, 9, 12, 16, 17, 18, 20,
25, 27, 28, 29 (top), 29 (bottom), 31, 32, 34, 36, 37, 38,
42 (top), 42 (bottom), 43, 44, 72, 73, 74, 75, 76, 77, 92,
94, 95, 96, 97, 102, 103, 104, 113, 114, 115, 116, 118,
119, 122, 123, 124, 128, 145, 146.

Photos on the following pages © Ariade / ESKA
Tijdschriften, Utrecht, The Netherlands: 13, 26, 30,
40, 41, 45, 46, 65, 66, 68 (left), 68 (right), 69 (top), 69
(bottom), 70, 89, 90, 91, 98 (top), 98 (bottom), 99 (top
left and right), 99 (bottom), 100, 101, 120, 121, 125,
126, 148, 150, 151.

Every effort has been made to ensure that all
information in this book is accurate. However, due to
differing conditions, yarns, and individual crocheting
skills, the publisher cannot be responsible for any
injuries, losses, or other damages which may result
from the use of the information in this book.

Printed and bound in Hong Kong.

For information on how you can have Better Homes
and Gardens delivered to your door, write to: Mr.
Robert Austin, P.O. Box 4536, Des Moines, IA 50336.

The Filet Crochet Book

Chris Rankin

With An Introduction By Nola Theiss

A Sterling/ **Lark** book
Sterling Publishing Co., Inc., New York

TABLE OF CONTENTS

Three identical window panels softly filter the morning light. The traditional floral motif creates an alluring pattern on the interior of the room. Passersby can admire the beautiful handwork. Welcome to the craft of filet crochet! (See page 64 for instructions)

AN INTRODUCTION TO FILET CROCHET

Filet is one of the simplest and most expressive forms of all crochet. It requires the knowledge of only a few simple stitches and the ability to follow a chart. Using filled and open squares to form an image or motif, filet crochet is actually a form of drawing with thread. Because of its simplicity, it is used extensively in Europe for such household items as curtains, towel and shelf edgings, doilies, and bed coverings. Because of its beauty, it is used to ornament functional items such as the addition of a filet crochet border to a pillow.

A precise history of crochet is elusive, although the conflicting reports of its origination make for interesting reading. Shards of clay with impressions of chained loops lead some historians to believe the Pima Indians in the American Southwest were the first crocheters. Early sailors who whiled away empty hours by making nets and knots, and Middle Eastern shepherds who used their spare time to manipulate grass, flax, and wool fibers are also credited with inventing crochet.

Etymological evidence points to three other possible inventors. The Scottish and Scandinavian words for crochet possibly originate from the word "crook," and might have been named after shepherds who used miniature versions of their herding crooks to make blankets (called "rugges") to keep themselves warm on cool nights. The word crochet also has French origins, dating back to lace-making nuns in the 13th through 19th centures who possibly used hooks to make some of their laces.

There are, however, three things one can say for sure about the history of crochet. First, many people did it, although the form was probably re-invented hundreds of times and used for a narrow purpose in each case. When it was no longer needed or desired, crochet disappeared, only to be invented again later. After all, what could be more basic than playing with string? Many children invent crochet every day.

Second, there is little physical evidence of early crochet because the few existent samples have all deteriorated so badly they can hardly be recognized. Most of the people who crocheted in earlier times

were the poor working class, and their products were hardly considered as art worth preserving.

Third, most languages of Europe and the Middle East are related; thus the word "crochet" means "hook" in some variation in almost any of these languages.

Thanks to the potato, the murky history of crochet becomes clearer. In the mid 1840s, the Irish famine (a two-year period when the main staple of the Irish diet, the potato, rotted in the fields) caused desperation among the poor. Before the famine, many Irish women had been earning extra money by knitting for the gentry. Nuns often organized these women and sold their products for them. As the plight of many families became more desperate, these nuns introduced and taught crocheting because it could imitate the appearance of European laces and be marketed for higher prices. As many of these Irish peasants emigrated to America, they brought their crochet skills to a new country.

Perhaps the most overpowering reason for crochet's popularity in the mid 1800s was that every other lady

6

Opposite page: Cotton tablecloth made by Anna Rundquist of Elgin, Illinois while awaiting the birth of her first child in 1876. The commemorative centennial filet patterns include: a large eagle, flags, a shield, and the dates 1776 - 1876. 95 inches by 78 inches.

Top: White cotton bedspread made in 1876 in celebration of the centennial and includes filet picture patterns of every United States president from 1776 - 1876. Artist unknown. 95½ inches by 78½ inches.

Below: White cotton bedspread with patriotic filet motifs to honor the 200th anniversary of George Washington's birth. Artist unknown. 95 inches by 78 inches.

All photos courtesy of the Smithsonian Institution, from the collection of the National Museum of History, political history and textile divisions.

was doing it. Queen Victoria, in an act of royal generosity, accepted gifts of Irish crocheted lace for her gowns, and the royalty of Europe quickly followed suit. (Queen Victoria learned to crochet herself and was often seen crocheting in public.) Books of crochet lace patterns were published in Europe and America and were wildly popular. American women's magazines such as "Godey's Lady's Book" were filled with crochet patterns. Special crochet thread was produced by enterprising textile manufacturers. During this peak in crochet's popularity, filet crochet was the favorite.

Historically, filet crochet has always used white cotton thread. Like most "facts" about crochet, there are many theories as to why it was done in white. The most popular is that white has a religious significance because of its association with holiness and purity. Since many of the motifs in 19th century filet crochet had religious symbolism — such as crosses and angels — and since it was first taught by nuns, this seems a logical theory.

Other reasons for the use of white can also be put forth. Cotton is naturally white, and dyeing is expensive. (If a color were desired, a white filet border could be sewn onto white fabric and dyed together for a perfect match.) Also, since many of the articles made of filet crochet are used as home decorations, and since white blends with all colors, the choice of white is a natural. Filet crochet doilies are often placed over dark wood or fabric, and the contrast of the filled and open squares is shown to full advantage if the thread is white. Curtains made in white filet crochet glow in the sunlight and stand out against a dark sky, and there is little problem with fading by using white thread. Filet crochet is also a form of lace, and lace has traditionally been white. Although a thousand other reasons could be put forth as to why filet crochet is white, perhaps the best reason is the one a tired mother gives to her child: "It just is."

7

The popularity of filet crochet is easy to explain. Unlike many other forms of crochet, filet crochet is highly individualistic. In a sense, it is like drawing in the air. Like a pencil drawing, it uses light and shadow to create an image where there was none before. A crocheter can take a sheet of graph paper and fill in squares to design a realistic or abstract filet image. Depending on the fineness of the thread and the size of the squares, the crocheter can create a detailed picture. By varying the amount of fill in each square, it is even possible to create the illusion of shadow and perspective.

During World War II, national contests were held in which patriotic themes were carefully "drawn" in filet crochet. Most of us probably remember going to our grandmother's house and finding doilies and table runners on every available surface. For many years, this look was considered somewhat old-fashioned, but today filet crochet is making a strong comeback. It has never gone out of style in Europe, and many of the styles seen there seem especially congruous with the popular American style of country decor.

The designs in this book have been chosen from the best designs in Europe, particularly from Germany and the Netherlands. As you walk through the streets of small towns in Holland, the diversity and beauty of the filet crochet curtains and valances in the windows is overwhelming. Themes of flowers and fruits, animals and birds, landscapes and pictorial scenes compete with abstract geometric and symbolic designs such as hearts and diamonds. Inside the homes, these window designs are duplicated and elaborated upon in doilies, wall hangings, tablecloths, and on bed linens of all description.

When an item is made entirely of filet crochet, it is often edged by a border which may incorporate other types of crochet such as picots. We have tried to be careful to select edgings which are not too difficult and which add to the beauty of the filet design. In a few designs, other stitches are used as part of the background, with the filet motif as the main part of the design. Specifically, there are a few designs which use V-arcs, which are really only variations of the filet crochet technique.

There are no techniques used in this book that are very difficult. We believe even a "non-crocheter" can quickly learn the stitches to create the simplest designs. Although increasing and decreasing at the edges requires some skill, the general directions which follow give a choice of methods to suit any crocheter. The simplicity of filet crochet is one of the reasons we think it has been popular for so many years and why it is experiencing such an increase in interest now.

An experienced filet crocheter's workbasket is filled with beautiful filet edgings, just waiting for the next appropriate usage: perhaps for a pillowcase, a favorite pillow, a cherished slip or for a festive tablecloth. The edging cascading out of the box is shown on page 26 as a shelf edging.

GENERAL DIRECTIONS

Filet crochet is a very simple technique. To make your crocheting life easy, we suggest you go to your local yarn store and buy a spool of white sewing thread in every weight you can find, and one ball of crochet cotton or anything resembling crochet cotton in each weight you can find. You will probably find that your choice of crochet thread is limited to D.M.C. or Coats and Clark and perhaps a European brand or two. These companies will often have several products of the same weight with different finishes. Buy one of each to use as gauge testers. These are not frivolous purchases, but part of your personal quality control lab. Besides, you can always make a doily out of the leftover thread. Also, buy a complete set of steel crochet hooks from size 14 to 000. Steel hooks are inexpensive, and there is nothing worse than not having the right size hook when you need it. You probably already have some plastic or aluminum hooks but they are too large for crochet thread. If you have a favorite crochet hook, figure out what it is you like about it. Does it have a comfortable thumb rest? Does it have a gradual or sharp taper from the hook to the shank? How blunt or pointed is the tip? Working with steel hooks is the same as working with plastic or aluminum hooks. Don't be too concerned about the steel hook splitting the thread as it will probably be more tightly twisted than yarn. Since some borders are actually worked into the fabric, the smallest hooks have to be pointed enough to penetrate fabric. Once you find a brand you like, buy a complete set, preferably with a case. It is easier to keep hooks from running away if they have a home to go to after they've finished work. Besides, one does feel professional with the proper tools.

There is a system to the sizing of threads which will be explained here, however, I have always found it very confusing. The theoretical size I want is never available or the thread which seems right is not marked for size. Threads are supposed to have a size number listed on the label. (Many don't because consumers don't know what the numbers mean.) The larger the number, the finer the thread. Since the finest steel hooks also have the largest number (14

HOW TO READ A FILET CROCHET CHART

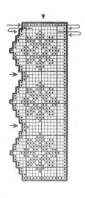 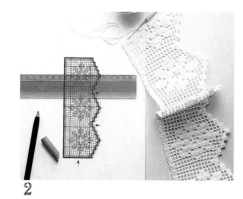 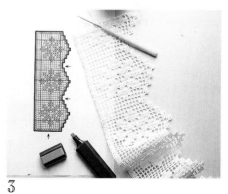

1

2

3

1. The chart shown the stitches as they appear on the right side of the work. Read the first line from right to left and crochet in that direction. Turn the work and follow the 2nd line from left to right and so on. For the pattern repeat work chart to the 2nd arrow shown at right edge on

this chart, then repeat the rows between the arrows as many times as desired. Finish the piece by completing the rows of chart above the 2nd arrow.

2. "Where am I on the chart?" After an interruption, it is easy to find your place if you have

placed a ruler under the row you are working on. Magnetic boards and markers are available for this purpose.

3. When working a large piece, it is a good idea to highlight the pattern repeat with a marker to help you find your place.

being the smallest hook), you can try to match your hook and thread numerically. The finest thread is size 100. It will take forever to find thread this fine, but the patience you develop looking for it will serve you well because it will take forever to make anything with it! In the ridiculously-fine category, there is also size 80 thread. Then there is size 50, which is equivalent to ordinary sewing thread.

Next comes size 8, then 5, then 3, then brand names which do not give a size indication but which look like crochet thread. You may hear the terms "fine count," "coarse count," "bedspread weight," "tatting thread," etc., all of which mean something to a specific manufacturer but there is no industry standard. You may also find a variety of finishes such as pearl, mercerized, sheen, and matte, as well as other categories such as cordonnet or cable. A few of the designs in the book can be made with fingering weight yarn or heavy cotton thread. There are also a variety of fiber blends available, although I can't see any reason for using anything but pure cotton. Be aware that some manufacturers make the same product and put different labels on it by region. Buy one of everything that appeals to you and experiment. Compared to other natural fibers, cotton thread is relatively cheap.

Now that you have set up your filet crochet lab, you are ready to make any of the designs in this book. Listed under the heading "Materials" in each set of directions, we have given the size hook recommended by the designer as well as the gauge necessary to make the design pictured. The amount of thread required is listed by grams, but obviously different brands have different yardages so buy more than you think you'll need. You can probably return it or put in in the proverbial oddball collection we all accumulate and use to make gifts of crocheted snowflakes someday. Since it is a given that filet crochet is white, we have not specified a color in the directions unless it is something other than white or has been dyed. If you do use a colored thread, be sure that all balls come from the same dye lot. We have not indicated a specific thread size since that depends on the final gauge you obtain. It will be necessary for you to experiment with the threads available to you.

The first rule for choosing thread is that it must fit in the hook. Once you have affirmed that, make a swatch at least 4" x 4" using the recommended size hook. Obviously, after a few rows you will know if you are way off or close to the mark. Adjust accordinging. If you can't get the exact gauge, you will have

to decide if you can live with a piece that is smaller or bigger than the original. You may find that the actual motif changes in proportion if the thread, hook, or tension changes.

Before you can begin testing the gauge for a given project, you'll need to know how to do filet crochet in the first place. Filet crochet is characterized by its open and filled squares. The filled squares are arranged in motifs. The motifs are usually worked by following charts wherein each motif square is represented by a square on the chart. Most filet crochet is worked in squares formed by parallel sides of one double crochet with a top and bottom made from 2 chain stitches. For this most common type of filet crochet, begin with a chain base which is always a multiple of 3 chain stitches for each square of the motif, plus one double crochet at the end. Thus, the original chain will be a multiple of 3 + 1. Each even row (one without increases or decreases) begins with a turning chain of 3 and ends by working the last double crochet in the third chain of the turning chain of the previous row. The instructions will indicate in which stitch counted from the hook you will insert the hook.

Here is how the designer figured that out: the first row after the foundation chain begins with a chain 3 for the outside edge of the first square. If it is an open square, 2 more chain stitches will have been allowed for the top, and the hook will be inserted in a stitch which allows for 2 chains at the bottom of the square. This means that to make an open square, you must insert the hook in the 8th chain from the hook. If the first square is filled, you still need 3 chain stitches for the outside double crochet. Insert the hook in the 4th chain from the hook, make one double crochet in the following 2 chain stitches. A filled square has 4 double crochet stitches: 1 at each edge and 2 in the center. The last double crochet of the square also serves as the first double crochet of the following square. Because there are 4 double crochets in each filled square, one of the double crochets serves a dual purpose, so in counting the number of stitches required, you only count 3 for each square, plus one to close the last square.

All filet squares are not created equal. For really large projects such as tablecloths or those which use a thick thread and hook, you make triple crochet stitches for the square outlines and fill. You may vary the number of chain stitches between the square edges as well. One-chain squares give a very dense appearance while 3-chain squares give a very open appearance. Some motifs have 2 chains between the squares, but in order to give some squares a less-filled appearance, only 1 double crochet is worked under the chain 2 arc, while other squares are filled with 2 double crochet stitches. A V-stitch may also be worked in filet squares which have 3 chain stitches. This is done by working 1 double crochet for the first side of the square, chaining 2, working 1 single crochet in the center chain, chaining 2, and then working 1 double crochet in the following stitch. These variations are explained in the patterns in which they are used.

Examples:
Here is a piece of filet crochet worked with 1 double crochet, chain 1; with 1 double crochet for an open square and 3 double crochet for a filled square. The last double crochet of 1 square is also the first double crochet of the following square.

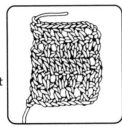

Next is a piece of filet crochet worked with 1 double crochet, chain 2; with 1 double crochet for an open square and 4 double crochet for a filled square. The last double crochet of one square is also the first double crochet of the following square.

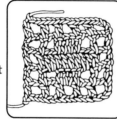

A NOTE ABOUT THE CHARTS
Since filet squares all blend into each other, the last st of 1 square is the first st of the next. Therefore, an isolated square may consist of 4 stitches (2 sides to the square and 2 stitches in the center), but on a chart, each square requires only 3 stitches because it will share its last stitch as the first stitch of the next square. There will be 1 stitch at the end of the row to close the last square. All the charts are accompanied by a Key to Chart which clearly explains the symbols used. Some of the charts use the international symbolcraft symbols or some version of them. We have included some of the most common ones here for your information, but you should really check the Key to Chart for the specific pattern you are working.

U.S.		British	
●	= Chain	●	= Chain
▼	= Slip stitch	▼	= Slip stitch or single crochet
T	= Single crochet	T	= Double crochet
‡	= Half double crochet	‡	= Treble crochet
‡	= Triple crochet	‡	= Double treble crochet

As you can see from the chart, the American and British terms are the same, but are off kilter by 1 stitch throughout.

Some of the charts are a little tricky because the design uses some unusual techniques to make an especially nice corner or some other clever and beautiful effect. These techniques are not really difficult, but may call for some creative thinking on your part. You may be told to make a corner by working in the top edge of one side of a piece to begin the next side. Look at the following sketch for an example of an unusual corner which requires you to turn the piece to form a corner.

A. This section is worked first and fastened off after Row 62 is completed. Then turn the piece so that the straight edge is horizontal and Row 62 is at the right.

B. Crocheting is resumed along the straight edge of the first piece. Rejoin the thread at the indicated arrow and work the first row in the edge squares. Work the remaining 2 corners in the same way, then sew the end of the 4th side to the beginning edge of the first piece.

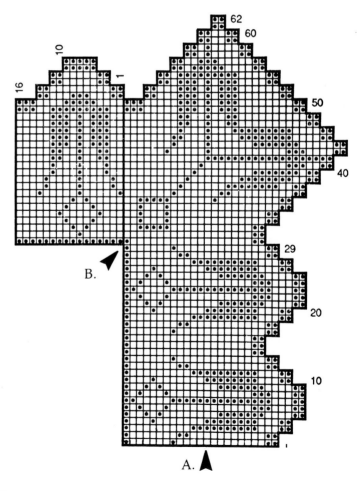

COMPARATIVE CROCHET HOOK SIZES

	ALUMINUM OR PLASTIC			STEEL		
U.S.	U.K.	Int'l (mm)		U.S.	U.K.	Int'l (mm)
	14	2	(small)	14	6	.6
	13			13	5½	
B	12	2.5		12	5	.75
C	11	3		11	4½	
D	10			10	4	1
E	9	3.5		9	3½	
F	8	4		8	3	1.25
G	7	4.5		7	2½	1.5
H	6	5		6	2	1.75
I	5	5.5		5	1½	
J	4	6		4	1	2
K	2	7		3	1/0	
				2	2/0	2.5
				1	3/0	3
				0		
			(large)	00		3.5

Try to think out why something is being done or even use paper or fabric cutouts to experiment. A few projects require an extra careful reading and a flexibilty of thinking about which is the top and which is the bottom of a piece. For pieces which begin or end with curves, it is often necessary to make the curves separately, then slip stitch them together and work across for the main part of the item.

The following instructions tell you how to shape the edges of pieces by increasing and decreasing. If you are a beginner, we suggest you begin with an even-sided piece to practice the basic technique, then move on to shaping. These instructions apply to filet crochet where an open square consists of 2 chain stitches between 2 double crochet stitches. If you are working with a larger or smaller number of stitches between the double crochet stitches, adapt the instructions accordingly. In most cases, if the designer wants you to use a different method or if the basic square is larger or smaller than the usual one, specific instructions will be given in the pattern. If they are not, use one of the following methods.

DECREASING AT THE BEGINNING
OF A ROW
Slip stitch across each stitch which you wish to decrease. If the following square is open, chain 5 in the first double crochet which will serve as the first double crochet and the top 2 chain

WHICH FILET PIECE IS THE MOST BEAUTIFUL

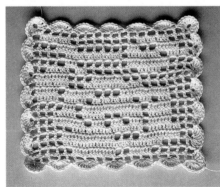

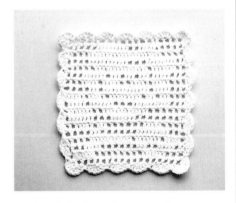

With thick yarn and only 1 chain stitch between the double crochet stitches, there is little contrast between the motif and the background.

Worked loosely and not blocked, the flower motif is wider and disproportionate. Tip: Use a smaller hook.

This filet piece is very nice. Worked tightly on a small hook, the squares are very even.

A GOOD FIRST PROJECT

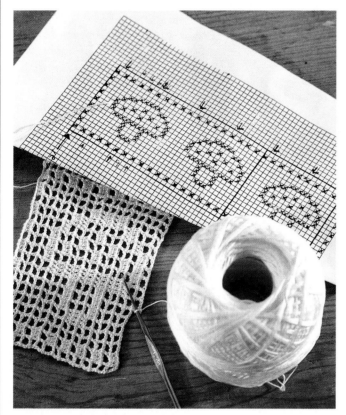

MUSHROOM VALANCE

SIZE
Approx. 8½" wide and 33" long.

MATERIALS
80 g white crochet cotton thread. 10 g each green and red crochet cotton thread. Steel crochet hook U.S. size 2. (U.K. size 2/0)

STITCHES USED
U.S. - Chain stitch (ch), single crochet (sc), double crochet (dc). U.K. - Chain stitch, double crochet, treble crochet.

GAUGE
9 squares in height and 11 squares in width = 4" x 4".

FILET CROCHET
Follow the chart. An open square = 1 dc, ch 2, skip 2 sts of previous row, 1 dc. A filled square = 4 dc. On the chart, the last st of 1 square serves as the first st of the foll square.

DIRECTIONS
Worked sideways. With white, ch 58 + ch 5 to turn (serves as first open square).

ROW 1: 1 dc in the 8th ch from the hook, 1 dc in each of the foll 3 ch, *ch 2, skip 2 sts, 1 dc in the foll 3 ch*, work * to * 8 times, ch 2, skip 2, 1 dc in the last ch. Continue by foll chart, beg with ch 5 for the first open square and ch 3 for the first dc of a filled square. Always work the last dc in the 3rd ch of the turning ch of previous row. Work 5 mushroom motifs or work to desired length, then work last 3 rows of chart. Fasten off. Along the lower edge, work as foll with red: in the corner st, *1 sc in the square, 1 picot (= ch 3, 1 sc in the 3rd ch from the hook)*, rep * to * across, end with 1 sc in the corner. Along the upper edge, work in green in the same manner as the lower edge, but in the 2nd square and every 9th square make a hanger by ch 15 in a picot, then work 1 sc in the 15th ch from the hook. Fasten off.

FINISHING
Pin piece to indicated measurement. Dampen and let dry. Mushroom edging: work chart same as valance, but use thinner crochet cotton and steel crochet hook U.S. size 6. (U.K. size 2)

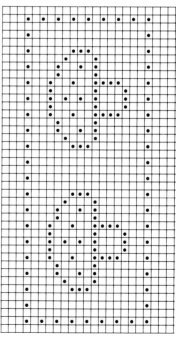

KEY TO CHART
□ = Open square
• = Filled square

stitches of the first square. For a filled square, chain 3, and then work 1 double crochet in the following double crochet stitches.

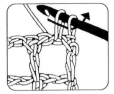  

DECREASING AT THE END OF A ROW

Work the desired number of stitches, turn the work, leaving the desired number of decreased stitches unworked at end of row. Continue as usual on the following row.

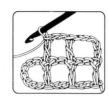

INCREASING AN OPEN SQUARE AT THE BEGINNING OF A ROW

To increase an open square at the beginning of a row, chain 7. (The first 2 chains form the lower edge of the new square; the following 3 chain stitches will serve as the double crochet; and the last 2 chain stitches will serve as the top of the new square.) Work 1 double crochet in the last double crochet of the previous row and continue across.

INCREASING A FILLED SQUARE AT THE BEGINNING OF A ROW

To increase a filled square at the beginning of a row, chain 5. (The first 2 chain stitches form the lower edge of the new square, and the following 3 chain stitches will serve as the double crochet.) Work 1 double crochet in the 4th and 5th chain from the hook, and work 1 double crochet in the last double crochet of the previous row.

INCREASING AN OPEN SQUARE AT THE END OF A ROW

Work as follows: chain 2, wrap the yarn around the hook twice, insert the hook under the last unworked double crochet, draw through a loop, *draw a loop through 2 loops on hook*, work * to * 3 times total.

INCREASING A FILLED SQUARE AT THE END OF A ROW

Work as follows: after the last stitch, wrap yarn around hook twice, insert hook under the last worked double crochet and draw through one loop. Yarn over, draw through 2 loops, yarn over, draw through 2 loops on hook twice more = 1 loop on hook.

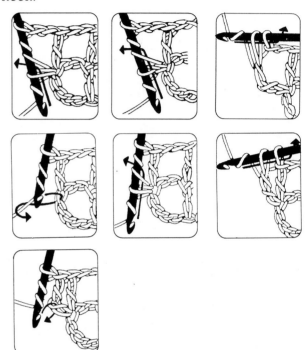

INCREASING AT CORNERS

Many of the patterns have two charts. One showing the filet work and another showing how to work the corner increases. A filled square will be increased by working a specified number of stitches under the arc in the corner stitch of the previous row. This will be shown on the chart. An open square will be worked by making more chain stitches than normal over the square. This will depend on whether you will be working over a filled or open square. The corner chart will show how many stitches to make in either case so the instructions will say something like, "Follow the corner chart for corner increases. For filled squares, follow row 2; for an open square follow row 1 or 3." Here is an example of a corner chart.

CORNER CHART

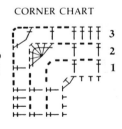

- = Ch
T = Sc
Ŧ = Dc

After you have finished your filet piece, you may wish to put an edging on the piece to round out increases or decreases or simply for decoration. If the edging is shown in the photo, the instructions will include an edging chart which can be followed. The most common edging is a picot stitch which is simple a number of chain stitches which are joined to the first chain with a slip stitch or single crochet. The instructions for a 3 ch picot will read: "ch 3, 1 sc in the 3rd chain from the hook." The picots may be separated by slip stitching or single crocheting across any space between them.

BLOCKING

Now that the piece is complete, you will need to block it. To do this, pin the piece to a towel to the finished measurements using large-headed, rust-proof pins. Spritz water on it and let dry. That's all.

SEWING INSETS AND EDGINGS

Sewing the filet piece onto fabric is usually done with white sewing thread and very fine stitches. Often you will be told to zigzag over the edges of fabric and then cover the hem with the filet piece. Or you may be asked to make a rolled hem, which is a very small doubled hem that is whipstitched in place.

One of the most beautiful hems is the doubled hem with mitered corners and openwork. We suggest you play paper cutouts with this one before you attempt the real thing. In most cases you will be making a 2" hem so you must allow 4 extra inches on each side of the fabric. Four inches from each edge on the wrong side of fabric, mark the wrong side of the fabric (this is the actual hemline), then 2" from the hemline

toward the outside edges, mark the second line —this is the first fold line. 2" from the hemline toward the inside, mark a 3rd line — this is where you will sew the hem down. You will have 3 lines of each edge and 9 squares in each corner.

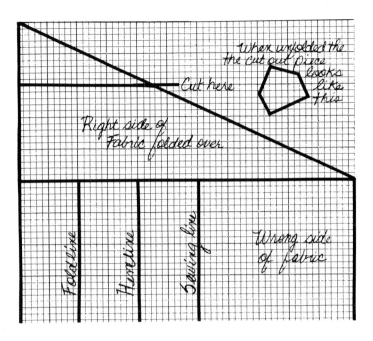

Now fold the fabric wrong sides together to form a point at the corner so that the fold bisects the corner.

Then cut the corner to form a point where the hemline meets at the corner. Open the fold, then fold fabric at the first line, fold again at the hemline. If you desire, you can make an openwork border above the hemline. To make an openwork border, you must be able to count the threads of the fabric. With a matching sewing thread, find a horizontal thread the desired distance from the top of the hem. Wrap sewing thread around 2 to 4 vertical threads of the fabric and pull tightly. Continue across, carefully following along the horizontal thread. You may have to adjust the number of threads to make the corner hole fall exactly at the corner. When sewing the hem, you may desire to wrap the hemming stitches around the openwork stitches as well.

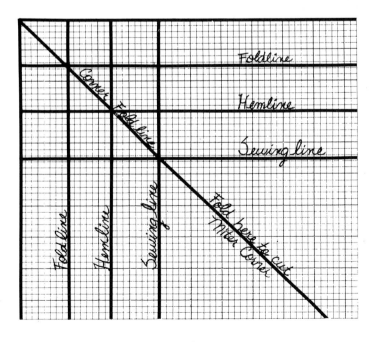

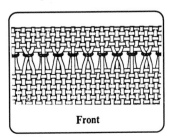
Front

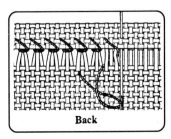
Back

PANELS AND DOILIES

Panels and doilies are ideal projects for beginners and make beautiful decorative accents around the home. They're also a good project to experiment with the effects of varying thread thicknesses and hook sizes.

Below, a snowflake motif is bordered first with a row of filet openwork and then with a traditional border pattern. (see page 22 for directions)

Right, designs from needlepoint patterns and children's coloring books can be adapted to a filet graph, made into a doily, and mounted under glass for a very personalized gift. (see page 22 for directions)

PANELS AND DOILIES

*A*nother way to use filet crochet panels and doilies is to place them over colorful serving plates and use them for table centerpieces.

When you tire of using them on your table, sew them together to make a filet sampler quilt or use them individually to make small pillows or insets.

Doilies and panels are great projects to discover how well you like filet crochet in colored thread instead of traditional white.

A variety of shapes and floral patterns is shown here. (see page 24 for directions)

A

B

PANELS AND DOILIES

These doilies and
panels are
crocheted around shaped
pieces of wire and
threaded with colorful
ribbon to make charm-
ing window accents.
They're small enough to
bring with you on trips
and visits, and are a
productive way to see if
you like a particular
pattern design.

The variety of designs
shown here — a clown,
a house, a rooster,
a bouquet of flowers,
a cat looking outdoors,
and a horseback rider
in the woods — illus-
trates the level of detail
you can achieve with
filet crochet. (see page
143 for directions)

INSTRUCTIONS FOR PANELS AND DOILIES

DOILY
See photo on page 16

SIZE
Doily approx. 11½" x 11½".

MATERIALS
100 g crochet cotton thread. Steel crochet hook U.S. size 6. (U.K. size 2)

STITCHES USED
U.S. - Chain stitch (ch), slip stitch (sl st), single crochet (sc), double crochet (dc). U.K. - Chain stitch, slip stitch, double crochet, treble crochet.

GAUGE
15 squares in height and width = 4" x 4".

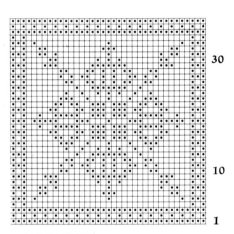

KEY TO CHART
□ = Open square
• = Filled square

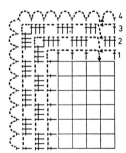

Border Chart

KEY TO CHART
▼ = Sl st
− = Ch
T = Sc
Ŧ = Dc

Both American and British stitches are listed under STITCHES USED in each pattern, however, only the American terms are used in the text. British readers should convert these instructions to British terms as they work the projects.

FILET CROCHET
Follow the chart. An open square = 1 dc, ch 2, skip 2 sts of previous row, 1 dc. A filled square = 4 dc. On the chart, the last st of 1 square serves as the first st of the foll square.

DIRECTIONS
Ch 111 + ch 3 to turn (serves as first dc).
ROW 1: Insert hook in the 4th ch from hook, then insert hook in each foll ch = 112 dc. Continue by foll chart, working rows 2 to 37. Beg each row with ch 3, then work last dc of row in the 3rd ch of turning ch of previous row. When filet chart is complete, work border chart. Beg rounds 1, 2 and 3 with ch 3, join each round with 1 sl st in the 3rd ch of turning ch. End the 4th round with 1 sl st in the first ch of previous round. Fasten off.

FINISHING
Pin piece to indicated measurement. Dampen and let dry.

WINDOW HANGING
See photo on page 17 A

SIZE
Hanging size approx. 10¼" x 8". Frame size approx. 11¾" x 14½".

MATERIALS
20 g crochet cotton thread. Steel crochet hook U.S. size 12. (U.K. size 5)

STITCHES USED
U.S. - Chain stitch (ch), triple crochet (tr). U.K. - Chain stitch, double treble crochet.

GAUGE
15 squares in height and width = 4" x 4".

FILET CROCHET
Follow the chart. An open square = 1 tr, ch 3, skip 3 sts of previous row, 1 tr. A partially filled square = 1 tr, ch 1, skip 1 st of previous row, 1 tr, skip 1 st of previous row, ch 1, 1 tr. A completely filled square = 4 tr. On the chart, the last st of 1 square serves as the first st of the foll square.

DIRECTIONS
Ch 161 + ch 4 to turn (serves as first tr).
ROW 1: 1 tr in the 7th ch from hook, then foll chart for 30 rows. Beg each row with ch 4. Always work the last tr of every row in the 4th ch of the turning ch of the previous row. Fasten off.

FINISHING
Pin piece to indicated measurement. Dampen and let dry.

See chart A on page 23

WINDOW HANGING
See photo on page 17 B

SIZE
Hanging size approx. 10" x 7¼". Frame size approx. 13¾" x 11½".

MATERIALS
10 g crochet cotton thread. Steel crochet hook U.S. size 12. (U.K. size 5)

STITCHES USED
U.S. - Chain stitch (ch), triple crochet (tr). U.K. - Chain stitch, double treble crochet.

GAUGE
15 squares in height and width = 4" x 4".

FILET CROCHET
Follow the chart. An open square = 1 tr, ch 3, skip 3 sts of previous row, 1 tr. A partially filled square = 1 tr, ch 1, skip 1 st of previous row, 1 tr, skip 1 st of previous row, ch 1, 1 tr. A completely filled square = 4 tr. On the chart, the last st of 1 square serves as the first st of the foll square.

DIRECTIONS
Ch 64 + ch 4 to turn.
ROW 1: 1 tr in the 5th ch from the hook, 1 tr in each ch st across row = 65 tr. Work rows 2 to 28 of chart, inc and dec as shown on chart. Work incs and decs as shown on chart. For rows without incs or decs, beg with ch 4, end with last tr in the 4th ch of the turning ch of the previous row. Fasten off.

FINISHING
Pin piece to indicated measurement. Dampen and let dry.

See chart B on page 23

WINDOW HANGING
See photo on page 17 C

SIZE
Hanging size approx. 9¼" x 9¼". Frame size approx. 13" x 13".

MATERIALS
20 g crochet cotton thread. Steel crochet hook U.S. size 12. (U.K. size 5)

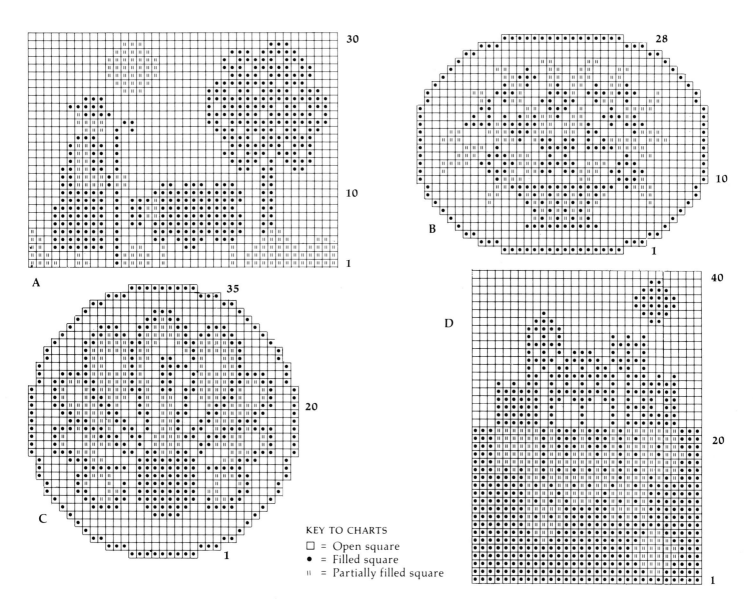

KEY TO CHARTS
- □ = Open square
- ● = Filled square
- ‖ = Partially filled square

STITCHES USED

U.S. - Chain stitch (ch), triple crochet (tr). U.K. - Chain stitch, double treble crochet.

GAUGE

15 squares in height and width = 4" x 4".

FILET CROCHET

Follow the chart. An open square = 1 tr, ch 3, skip 3 sts of previous row, 1 tr. A partially filled square = 1 tr, ch 1, skip 1 st of previous row, 1 tr, skip 1 st of previous row, ch 1, 1 tr. A completely filled square = 4 tr. On the chart, the last st of 1 square serves as the first st of the foll square.

DIRECTIONS

Ch 36 + ch 4 to turn (serves as first tr).

ROW 1: 1 tr in the 5th ch from the hook, 1 tr in each ch st across = 37 tr. Then follow chart for 35 rows. Work incs and decs as shown on chart. For rows without incs or decs, beg with ch 4, end with last tr in the 4th ch of the turning ch of the previous row. Fasten off.

FINISHING

Pin piece to indicated measurement. Dampen and let dry.

See chart C

WINDOW HANGING
See photo on page 17 D

SIZE

Hanging size approx. 8" x 10¼". Frame size approx. 11½" x 13¾".

MATERIALS

20 g crochet cotton thread. Steel crochet hook U.S. size 12. (U.K. size 5)

STITCHES USED

U.S. - Chain stitch (ch), triple crochet (tr). U.K. - Chain stitch, double treble crochet.

GAUGE

15 squares in height and width = 4" x 4".

FILET CROCHET

Follow the chart. An open square = 1 tr, ch 3, skip 3 sts of previous row, 1 tr. A partially filled square = 1 tr, ch 1, skip 1 st of previous row, 1 tr, skip 1 st of

23

previous row, ch 1, 1 tr. A completely filled square = 4 tr. On the chart, the last st of 1 square serves as the first st of the foll square.

DIRECTIONS

Ch 120 + ch 4 to turn (serves as first tr).
ROW 1: 1 tr in the 5th ch from the hook, then 1 tr in each ch st across = 121 tr, then follow chart for 40 rows. Beg each row with ch 4. Always work the last tr of every row in the 4th ch of the turning ch of the previous row. Fasten off.

FINISHING

Pin piece to indicated measurement. Dampen and let dry.

See chart D on page 23

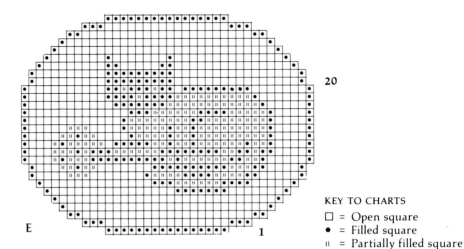

E   1   20

WINDOW HANGING,

See photo on page 17 E

SIZE

Hanging size approx. 10" x 7¼". Frame size approx. 13¾" x 11½".

MATERIALS

10 g crochet cotton thread. Steel crochet hook U.S. size 12. (U.K. size 5)

STITCHES USED

U.S. - Chain stitch (ch), triple crochet (tr). U.K. - Chain stitch, double treble crochet.

GAUGE

15 squares in height and width = 4" x 4".

FILET CROCHET

Follow the chart. An open square = 1 tr, ch 3, skip 3 sts of previous row, 1 tr. A

partially filled square = 1 tr, ch 1, skip 1 st of previous row, 1 tr, skip 1 st of previous row, ch 1, 1 tr. A completely filled square = 4 tr. On the chart, the last st of 1 square serves as the first st of the foll square.

DIRECTIONS

Ch 64 + ch 4 to turn (serves as first tr).
ROW 1: 1 tr in the 5th ch from the hook, then 1 tr in each ch across = 16 filled squares. Follow chart for 28 rows. Work incs and decs as shown on chart. For rows without incs or decs, beg with ch 4, end with last tr in the 4th ch of the turning ch of the previous row. Fasten off.

FINISHING

Pin piece to indicated measurement. Dampen and let dry.

See chart E

DOILY

See photo on page 18 A

SIZE

Approx. 11¾" x 11".

MATERIALS

30 g crochet cotton thread. Steel crochet hook U.S. size 10. (U.K. size 4)

STITCHES USED

U.S. - Chain stitch (ch), double crochet (dc). U.K. - Chain stitch, treble crochet.

GAUGE

21 squares x 23 rows = 4" x 4".

FILET CROCHET

Follow the chart. An open square = 1 dc, ch 2, skip 2 sts of previous row, 1 dc. A filled square = 4 dc. On the chart, the last st of 1 square serves as the first st of the foll square.

DIRECTIONS

Ch 189 + ch 3 to turn (serves as first dc).
ROW 1: 1 dc in the 4th, 5th, and 6th ch from the hook, (= 1 filled square). Continue by foll chart = 63 squares. Continue by foll chart from rows 2 to 32, then work rows 31 to 1. Beg each row with ch 3 and always work the last dc in the 3rd ch of the turning ch of previous row. Fasten off.

FINISHING

Pin pieces to indicated measurement. Dampen and let dry.

KEY TO CHART

□ = Open square
• = Filled square

KEY TO CHARTS

□ = Open square
• = Filled square
‖ = Partially filled square

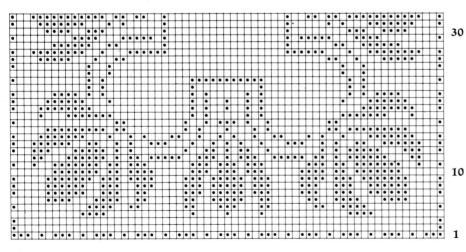

A   1   10   30

Instructions continued on page 141

BORDERS AND EDGINGS

Shelf edgings are a simple way to add charm and beauty to kitchen and dining areas. Although they make elegant additions to cabinets filled with heirloom china, don't be afraid to decorate the shelves of your everyday dishes with filet edgings.

The filet edging **below** uses a simple repeating snowflake motif. (see page 47 for directions)

Any favorite hobby, collection, or motif can be converted to a filet crochet pattern by tracing the outline of the item from a magazine or catalog and then converting your tracing to a graph.

BORDERS AND EDGINGS

Another way to use shelf edgings is to sew them to a length of fabric that's slightly wider than your shelf.

As **shown below**, the fabric makes a decorative lining for the shelf and eliminates the need for frequent dusting. (see page 47 for directions)

The casual dish cabinet, **right**, illustrates the versatility of filet crochet shelf edgings. (see page 47 for directions)

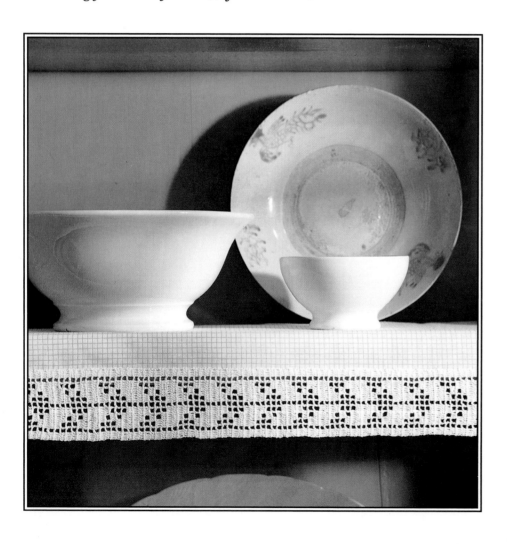

BORDERS AND EDGINGS

A modified version of the popular snowflake pattern, **left**, is equally complementary to a cabinet of formal dishware. (see page 48 for directions) The speed and simplicity of filet crochet makes it easy to replace your snowflake edgings with tulip or maple leaf edgings as the seasons change.

The colors and patterns you choose for your shelf edgings can be tailored to the existing decor of your home as shown **top right**. The pattern can also be repeated on small accessories such as potholders. (see page 48 for directions)

A star-spangled shelf edging, **bottom right**, makes a big splash in the bathroom linen closet. (see page 49 for directions) Page 97 features another project with this same pattern.

BORDERS AND EDGINGS

The delicacy of filet crochet makes it a beautiful accent for shelf edgings in the baby's room, and using traditional white crochet thread eliminates worries about whether to decorate in pink or blue.

Below, an unfinished storage shelf is easily decorated with a filet edging sewn to a floral print fabric. (see page 49 for directions) This pattern is also used for a baby's sheet panel (see page 101).

Other favorite baby motifs, such as animals and toy trains, ***shown right***, make unique edgings for sheets, curtains, and bassinette ruffles. (see pages 49 - 51 for directions) Since filet edgings will often

outlast the items they're attached to, they can be removed and reused or packed away into a box of baby mementos.

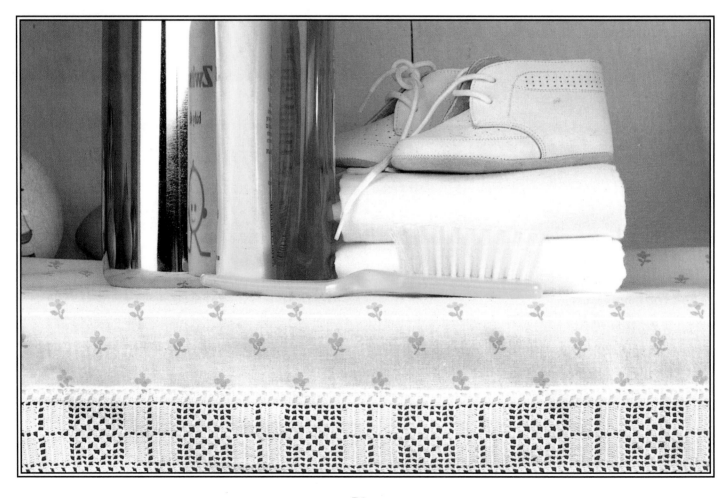

30

E

BORDERS AND EDGINGS

F ilet edgings also make beautiful embellishments for handkerchiefs and pocket linens. Using a smaller crochet hook and thinner thread makes the edgings compatible with the lightweight fabrics traditionally used for handkerchiefs.

Pictured here is a filet designer's worktable covered with a variety of geometric edging patterns. (see pages 51 53 for directions)

These same edgings can be made in wider strips and used as insets or borders for lingerie or for linens for formal table settings.

BORDERS AND EDGINGS

These colorful handkerchiefs with floral motif filet edgings serve as cheerful reminders of the beauty of spring. (see pages 53 - 55 for directions)

The delicate, lacy look of these edgings is achieved by the thinness of the thread and a plentiful use of unfilled filet squares.

As with the edgings on the previous page, these patterns can be lengthened and used to embellish lingerie or for linens for formal table settings.

A

BORDERS AND EDGINGS

A pocket handkerchief with a geometric filet pattern and cut corners, **shown left**, adds a very contemporary look while showcasing a very traditional talent. (see page 56 for directions)

Right, another geometric filet edging, this time made with a heavier crochet thread, attaches simply to a small square of cotton to make an attractive table napkin. (see page 57 for directions)

Cleaning is as simple as a cold water wash and a light pressing with starch.

BORDERS AND EDGINGS

S*hown here, an array of delicate filet patterns offers endless potential. Use them for borders on slips, cuffs on robes, insets on nightgowns, and top borders for lingerie bags.*

Varying in patterns from geometric shapes to soft garlands of roses, these projects are testimony to the well-guarded secret among filet crocheters: It looks so hard but it's really so easy! (see pages 57 - 60 for directions)

These filet crochet edgings would be an inexpensive but beautiful way to coordinate a bride's wedding trousseau.

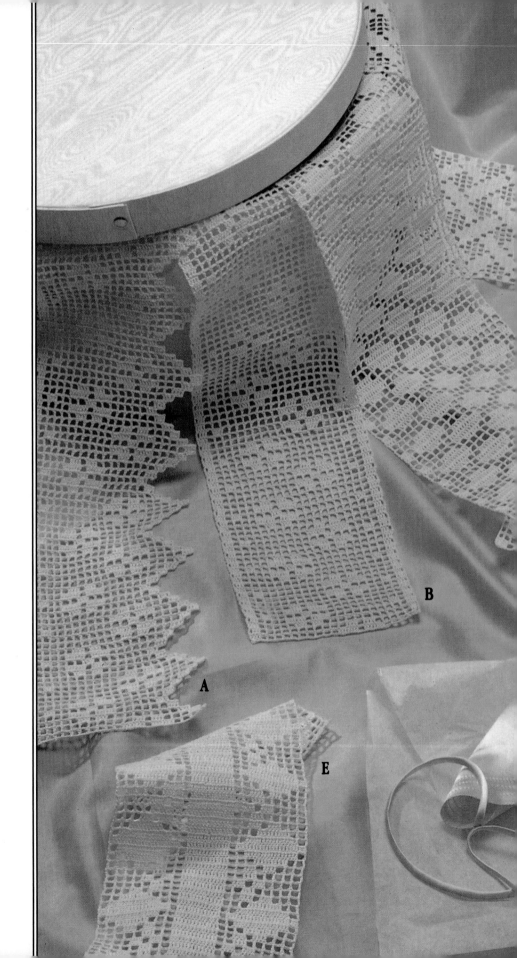

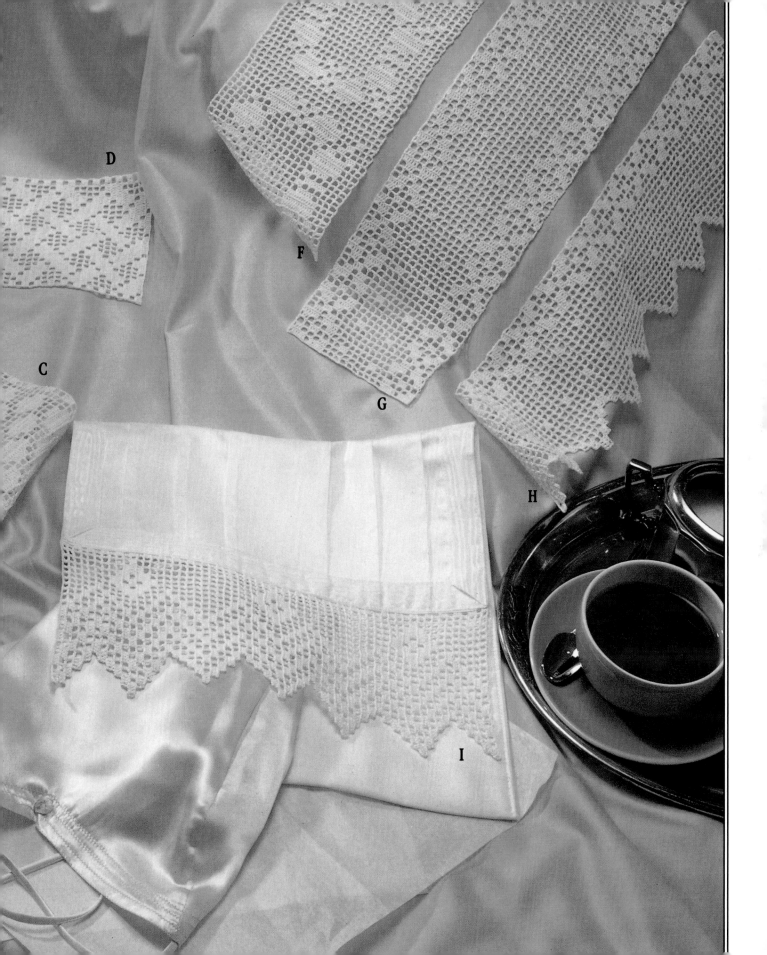

BORDERS AND EDGINGS

Filet crochet edgings also make beautiful borders for summer skirts and dresses.

The edging shown here uses a repeating rosebud and leaves motif. (see page 60 for directions)

The width of the edging can easily be adjusted by adding extra rows of open filet squares, and patterns from other filet projects in this book can be borrowed to create a wide variety of designs.

A skirt edging can be made in colored crochet thread to complement the colors of the dress or made in white and dipped in dye after it's been attached to the dress.

BORDERS AND EDGINGS

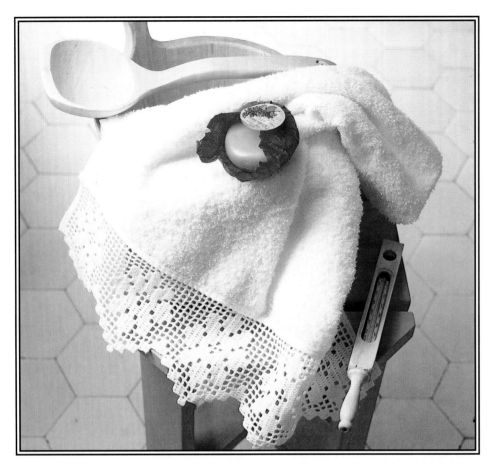

Filet crochet edgings also add a touch of elegance to your bathroom towels. The edgings are sewn to one end of the towel and will endure as many machine washings as the towel.

The edgings can be made in traditional white or in colors to match a bathroom's decor.

Top left, a repeating snowflake pattern adorns an off-white towel. (see page 61 for directions) **Bottom left**, a white filet crochet edging adds a summery look to an ordinary blue and white towel. (see page 61 for directions) **Right**, a thin strip of filet crochet makes an unusual inset in a towel. The geometric pattern is then repeated as a border. (see page 62 for directions)

BORDERS AND EDGINGS

I*f you've grown bored with your plain white curtains, spice them up with edgings of filet crochet.*

*The edgings can be placed both horizontally and vertically, like the diamond and zigzag motifs **shown left**. (see page 62 for directions)*

*The edgings can also be placed in horizontal rows as insets to invite extra sunshine indoors. (see page 63 for directions) As **shown right**, the motifs can be changed from row to row.*

BORDERS AND EDGINGS

This delicate filet crochet edging is a beautiful accent to an ordinary tablecloth and makes an ideal beginner's project. (see page 63 for directions) The same pattern can be used to make borders for table linens or tied into bows to make napkin rings.

If you'd prefer a wider edging, simply repeat additional rows of the chart until you're satisfied with the result.

INSTRUCTIONS FOR BORDERS AND EDGINGS

SHELF EDGING
See photo on page 25

SIZE
Approx. 6" wide. Each pat repeat is approx. 4¾".

MATERIALS
Crochet cotton thread. Steel crochet hook U.S. size 7. (U.K. size 2.5)

STITCHES USED
U.S. - Chain stitch (ch), double crochet (dc). U.K. - chain stitch, treble crochet.

GAUGE
12 squares x 13 rows = 4" x 4".

FILET CROCHET
Follow the chart. An open square = 1 dc, ch 2, skip 2 sts of previous row, 1 dc. A filled square = 4 dc. On the chart, the last st of 1 square serves as the first st of the foll square.

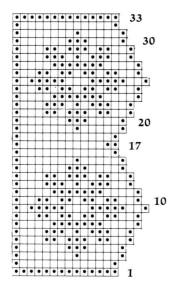

KEY TO CHART
□ = Open square
• = Filled square

DIRECTIONS
Ch 42 + ch 3 to turn.
ROW 1: Insert hook in the 4th ch from the hook and work 1 dc, work 1 dc in each ch across = 42 dc + 1 turning ch. Beg rows without inc or dec with ch 3 and end with 1 dc in each row in the 3rd ch of the turning ch of the previous row. Work inc and dec as shown on chart. Work rows 1 to 7, rep rows 2 to

17 to desired length, end with rows 18 to 33. Fasten off.

FINISHING
Pin piece to indicated measurement. Dampen and let dry.

SHELF EDGING
See photo on page 26

SIZE
2½" wide.

MATERIALS
50 g crochet cotton thread. Steel crochet hook U.S. size 8. (U.K. size 3)

STITCHES USED
U.S. - Chain stitch (ch), double crochet (dc). U.K. - chain stitch, treble crochet.

GAUGE
19 rows = 4".

FILET CROCHET
Follow the chart. An empty square = 1 dc, ch 2, skip 2 sts of previous row, 1 dc. A filled square = 4 dc. On the chart, the last st of 1 square serves as the first st of the foll square.

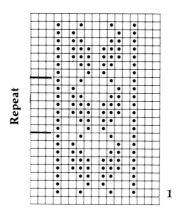

KEY TO CHART
□ = Open square
• = Filled square

DIRECTIONS
Work sideways. Ch 34 + ch 3 (serves as first dc).
ROW 1: 1 dc in the 5th ch from the hook, 1 dc in the foll 2 ch (= 1 filled square), *ch 2, skip 2, 1 dc in the foll ch*, work * to * twice, 1 dc in the foll 3 ch, work * to * 3 times, 1 dc in foll 3 ch, work * to *

twice, 1 dc in the foll 3 ch.
ROW 2: Ch 3, 1 dc in the foll 3 dc, work * to * 3 times, 1 dc in the foll 3 ch, ch 2, skip 2, 1 dc in the foll dc, 1 dc in the foll 3 ch, work * to * 3 times, 1 dc in each of the foll 3 dc. Continue by foll chart. Turn and beg every row with ch 3 which serves as the first dc of the first filled square. Work to desired length. Fasten off.

FINISHING
Pin piece to indicated measurement. Dampen and let dry.

SHELF EDGING
See photo on page 27

SIZE
Approx. width 4¼" wide. Each pat repeat is approx. 3½".

MATERIALS
100 g crochet cotton thread. Steel crochet hook U.S. size 8. (U.K. size 3)

STITCHES USED
U.S. - Chain stitch (ch), single crochet (sc), double crochet (dc). U.K. - chain stitch, double crochet, treble crochet.

GAUGE
16 squares x 19 rows = 4" x 4".

FILET CROCHET
Follow the chart. An open square = 1 dc, ch 2, skip 2 sts of previous row, 1 dc. A filled square = 4 dc. On the chart, the last st of 1 square serves as the first st of the foll square.

DIRECTIONS
Ch 42 + ch 3 to turn (serves as first dc).
ROW 1: 1 dc in the 4th ch from the hook, 1 dc in each of the foll ch = 43 dc. Continue by foll chart from rows 2 to 16, then work rows 17 to 32, 3 times, end with rows 33 to 49. Beg each row without incs or decs with ch 3 and always work the last dc in the 3rd ch of

Both American and British stitches are listed under STITCHES USED in each pattern, however, only the American terms are used in the text. British readers should convert these instructions to British terms as they work the projects.

the turning ch of previous row. Work inc and dec as shown on chart. Fasten off.

FINISHING

Pin piece to indicated measurement. Dampen and let dry.

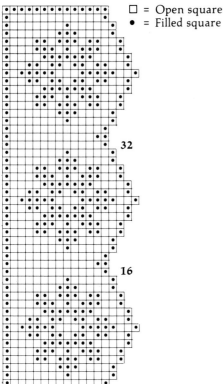

KEY TO CHART

□ = Open square
• = Filled square

SHELF EDGING

See photo on page 28

SIZE
4¼" wide.

MATERIALS
20 g crochet cotton thread for each 27" of edging. Steel crochet hook U.S. size 12. (U.K. size 5)

STITCHES USED
U.S. - Chain stitch (ch), single crochet (sc), double crochet (dc). U.K. - chain stitch, double crochet, treble crochet.

GAUGE
18 squares x 28 rows = 4" x 4".

FILET CROCHET
Follow the chart. An open square = 1 dc, ch 2, skip 2 sts of previous row, 1 dc. A filled square = 4 dc. Squares with V's = 1 dc, ch 2, 1 sc under the ch 2 of previous row, ch 2. On the chart, the last st of 1

square serves as the first st of the foll square.

DIRECTIONS
Ch 52 + ch 3 to turn (serves as first dc). ROW 1: 1 dc in the 4th ch from the hook, then foll the chart. Each row without incs or decs beg with ch 3 which counts as the first dc. Work rows 2 to 33 until desired length. Work increases and decreases as shown on chart. Fasten off.

FINISHING
Pin piece to indicated measurement. Dampen and let dry.

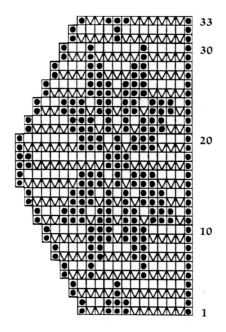

KEY TO CHART

V = Ch 2, 1 sc under the ch 2 of previous row, ch 2. (Always preceded and followed by 1 dc).
□ = Ch 3, skip 3 sts, 1 dc in the foll st.
• = 1 dc in each of 4 dc of the previous row.

SHELF EDGING

See photo on page 29, top

SIZE
4¾" x 23½" wide.

MATERIALS
Approx. 50 g blue crochet cotton thread. Steel crochet hook U.S. size 4. (U.K. size 1)

STITCHES USED
U.S. - Chain stitch (ch), slip stitch (sl st), single crochet (sc), double crochet (dc).

U.K. - chain stitch, slip stitch, double crochet, treble crochet.

GAUGE
12 squares in height and width = 4" x 4".

FILET CROCHET
Follow the chart. An open square = 1 dc, ch 2, skip 2 sts of previous row, 1 dc. A filled square = 4 dc. On the chart, the last st of 1 square serves as the first st of the foll square.

DIRECTIONS
Ch 36 + ch 3 to turn (serves as first dc). ROW 1: 1 dc in the 4th ch from the hook, 1 dc in next 2 ch, *ch 2, skip 2 ch, 1 dc*, rep * to * 10 times. In the last 3 ch, work 1 dc in each ch = 12 squares. Continue by foll chart rep rows 2 to 12, work between arrows 5 times, then work rows 13 to 21 once. Beg each row without incs or decs with ch 3 and always work the last dc in the 3rd ch of the turning ch of previous row. Work inc and dec as shown on chart. Work 1 row of sc with picots along top edge. Fasten off.

FINISHING
Pin pieces to indicated measurement. Dampen and let dry.

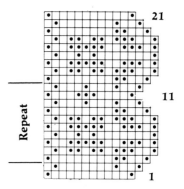

KEY TO CHART

□ = Open square
• = Filled square

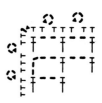

- = Ch   † = Dc
▲ = Sl st
T = Sc   ✪ = Picot: Ch 3, sl st in first ch

SHELF EDGING

See photo on page 29, bottom

SIZE

Approx. 6" wide. Each pat repeat is approx. 14½".

MATERIALS

Crochet cotton thread. Steel crochet hook U.S. size 7. (U.K. size 2.5)

STITCHES USED

U.S. - Chain stitch (ch), double crochet (dc). U.K. - chain stitch, treble crochet.

GAUGE

12 squares x 13 rows = 4" x 4".

FILET CROCHET

Follow the chart. An open square = 1 dc, ch 2, skip 2 sts of previous row, 1 dc. A filled square = 4 dc. On the chart, the last st of 1 square serves as the first st of the foll square.

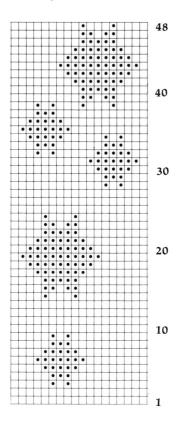

KEY TO CHART

□ = Open square
● = Filled square

DIRECTIONS

Ch 56 + ch 3 to turn.
ROW 1: Insert hook in the 8th ch from

hook and work 1 dc, continue by foll chart = 18 open squares. Beg rows with ch 3 and end with 1 dc in each row in the 3rd ch of the turning ch of the previous row. Work rows 1 to 48. Fasten off.

FINISHING

Pin piece to indicated measurement. Dampen and let dry.

SHELF EDGING

See photo on page 30

For Baby Sheet Panel, see photo on page 101

SIZE

1¾" wide.

MATERIALS

50 g crochet cotton yarn. Steel crochet hook U.S. size 12. (U.K. size 5)

STITCHES USED

U.S. - Chain stitch (ch), slip stitch (sl st), double crochet (dc). U.K. - chain stitch, slip stitch, treble crochet.

GAUGE

7 squares x 8 rows = ¾".

FILET CROCHET

Follow the chart. An open square = 1 dc, ch 2, skip 2 sts of previous row, 1 dc. A filled square = 4 dc. On the chart, the last st of 1 square serves as the first st of the foll square.

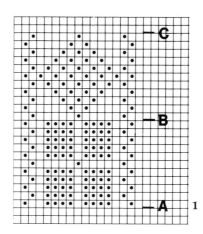

KEY TO CHART

□ = Open square
● = Filled square

DIRECTIONS

Work by foll chart, beg with point A. Ch 46 + ch 3. Beg at point A.

ROW 1: 1 dc in the 5th ch from the hook, 1 dc in the foll 2 ch, *ch 2, skip 2 ch, 1 dc in the foll ch*, work * to * twice, 1 dc in each of the foll 12 ch, work * to * once, 1 dc in each of the foll 12 ch, work * to * twice, 1 dc in each of the foll 3 ch sts. Continue by working the chart. At the end of every row, turn and ch 3 for the first dc of the first filled square and ch 5 for the first open square. Work chart from points A to C to desired length. Fasten off. If you desire a wider piece use a thicker yarn and larger hook.

FINISHING

Pin piece to indicated measurement. Dampen and let dry. (May also be used as baby sheet panel. When making baby sheet panel, pin to sheet as shown on photo on page 101 and sew on to sheet.)

BABY EDGING

See photo on page 31 A

SIZE

Approx. 4¼" wide.

MATERIALS

For every 37", 50 g crochet cotton thread. Steel crochet hook U.S. size 10. (U.K. size 4)

STITCHES USED

U.S. - Chain stitch (ch), slip stitch (sl st), double crochet (dc). U.K. - chain stitch, slip stitch, treble crochet.

GAUGE

21 squares = 4¼" wide.

FILET CROCHET

Follow the chart. An open square = 1 dc, ch 2, skip 2 sts of previous row, 1 dc. A filled square = 4 dc. On the chart, the last st of 1 square serves as the first st of the foll square.

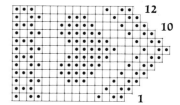

KEY TO CHART

□ = Open square
● = Filled square

DIRECTIONS

Ch 45 + ch 3 to turn.
ROW 1: Insert hook in the 4th ch from

hook and work 1 dc, work 1 dc in the 5th and 6th ch from hook, work by foll chart = 15 squares. Beg each row without incs or decs with ch 3 and end with 1 dc in each row in the 3rd ch of the turning ch of the previous row. Rep the 12 rows of pat chart to desired length. Work inc and dec as shown on chart. Fasten off.

FINISHING
Pin piece to indicated measurement. Dampen and let dry.

BABY EDGING
See photo on page 31 B

SIZE
Approx. 3½" wide.

MATERIALS
For every 37", 50 g crochet cotton thread. Steel crochet hook U.S. size 10. (U.K. size 4)

STITCHES USED
U.S. - Chain stitch (ch), slip stitch (sl st), double crochet (dc). U.K. - chain stitch, slip stitch, treble crochet.

GAUGE
16 squares = 3½" wide.

FILET CROCHET
Follow the chart. An open square = 1 dc, ch 2, skip 2 sts of previous row, 1 dc. A filled square = 4 dc. On the chart, the last st of 1 square serves as the first st of the foll square.

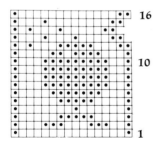

KEY TO CHART
□ = Open square
• = Filled square

DIRECTIONS
Ch 48 + ch 3 to turn.
ROW 1: Insert hook in the 4th ch from hook and work 1 dc, work 1 dc in the 5th and 6th ch from hook, work by foll chart = 16 squares. Beg each row without incs or decs with ch 3 and end each row with 1 dc in each row in the

3rd ch of the turning ch of the previous row. Rep the 16 rows of pat chart to desired length. Fasten off.

FINISHING
Pin piece to indicated measurement. Dampen and let dry.

BABY EDGING
See photo on page 31 C

SIZE
Approx. 4" wide.

MATERIALS
For every 35½", 50 g crochet cotton thread. Steel crochet hook U.S. size 10. (U.K. size 4)

STITCHES USED
U.S. - Chain stitch (ch), slip stitch (sl st), double crochet (dc). U.K. - chain stitch, slip stitch, treble crochet.

GAUGE
18 squares = 4" wide.

FILET CROCHET
Follow the chart. An open square = 1 dc, ch 2, skip 2 sts of previous row, 1 dc. A filled square = 4 dc. On the chart, the last st of 1 square serves as the first st of the foll square.

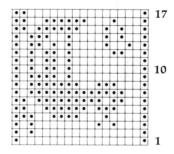

KEY TO CHART
□ = Open square
• = Filled square

DIRECTIONS
Ch 54 + ch 3 to turn.
ROW 1: Insert hook in the 4th ch from hook and work 1 dc, work 1 dc in the 5th and 6th ch from hook, then work by foll chart = 18 squares. Beg each row with ch 3 and end with 1 dc in each row in the 3rd ch of the turning ch of the previous row. Rep the 17 rows of pat chart to desired length. Fasten off.

FINISHING
Pin piece to indicated measurement. Dampen and let dry.

BABY EDGING
See photo on page 31 D

SIZE
Approx. 4" wide.

MATERIALS
For every 35½", 50 g crochet cotton thread. Steel crochet hook U.S. size 10. (U.K. size 4)

STITCHES USED
U.S. - Chain stitch (ch), slip stitch (sl st), double crochet (dc). U.K. - chain stitch, slip stitch, treble crochet.

GAUGE
19 squares = 4" wide.

FILET CROCHET
Follow the chart. An open square = 1 dc, ch 2, skip 2 sts of previous row, 1 dc. A filled square = 4 dc. On the chart, the last st of 1 square serves as the first st of the foll square.

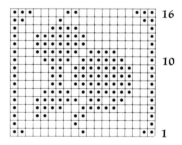

KEY TO CHART
□ = Open square
• = Filled square

DIRECTIONS
Ch 57 + ch 3 to turn.
ROW 1: Insert hook in the 4th ch from hook and work 1 dc, work 1 dc in the 5th and 6th ch from hook, then work by foll chart = 19 squares. Beg each row with ch 3 and end with 1 dc in each row in the 3rd ch of the turning ch of the previous row. Rep the 16 rows of pat chart to desired length. Fasten off.

FINISHING
Pin piece to indicated measurement. Dampen and let dry.

BABY EDGING
See photo on page 31 E

SIZE
Approx. 4" wide.

MATERIALS
For every 35½", 50 g crochet cotton

thread. Steel crochet hook U.S. size 10. (U.K. size 4)

STITCHES USED

U.S. - Chain stitch (ch), slip stitch (sl st), double crochet (dc). U.K. - chain stitch, slip stitch, treble crochet.

GAUGE

18 squares = 4″ wide.

FILET CROCHET

Follow the chart. An open square = 1 dc, ch 2, skip 2 sts of previous row, 1 dc. A filled square = 4 dc. On the chart, the last st of 1 square serves as the first st of the foll square.

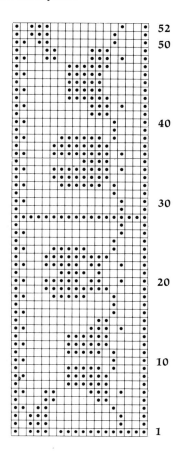

KEY TO CHART

□ = Open square
● = Filled square

DIRECTIONS

Ch 54 + ch 3 to turn.
ROW 1: Insert hook in the 4th ch from hook and work 1 dc, work 1 dc in the 5th and 6th ch from hook, then work by foll chart = 18 squares. Beg each row with ch 3 and end with 1 dc in each row in the 3rd ch of the turning ch of the

previous row. Rep the 52 rows of pat chart to desired length. Fasten off.

FINISHING

Pin piece to indicated measurement. Dampen and let dry.

BABY EDGING

See photo on page 31 F

SIZE

Approx. 3½″ wide.

MATERIALS

For every 35½″, 50 g crochet cotton thread. Steel crochet hook U.S. size 10. (U.K. size 4)

STITCHES USED

U.S. - Chain stitch (ch), slip stitch (sl st), double crochet (dc). U.K. - chain stitch, slip stitch, treble crochet.

GAUGE

17 squares = 3½″ wide.

KEY TO CHART

□ = Open square
● = Filled square

FILET CROCHET

Follow the chart. An open square = 1 dc, ch 2, skip 2 sts of previous row, 1 dc. A filled square = 4 dc. On the chart, the last st of 1 square serves as the first st of the foll square.

DIRECTIONS

Ch 51 + ch 3 to turn.
ROW 1: Insert hook in the 4th ch from hook and work 1 dc, work 1 dc in the 5th and 6th ch from hook, then work by foll chart = 17 squares. Beg each row with ch 3 and end with 1 dc in each row in the 3rd ch of the turning ch of the previous row. Rep the 57 rows of pat chart to desired length. Fasten off.

FINISHING

Pin piece to indicated measurement. Dampen and let dry.

HANDKERCHIEF EDGING

See photo on page 32 A

SIZE

Approx. 1¼″ wide.

MATERIALS

15 g crochet cotton thread. Steel crochet hook U.S. size 14. (U.K. size 6) 1 handkerchief 9¾″ x 9¾″.

STITCHES USED

U.S. - Chain stitch (ch), slip stitch (sl st), single crochet (sc), double crochet (dc). U.K. - chain stitch, slip stitch, double crochet, treble crochet.

GAUGE

14 squares x 14 rows = 4″ x 4″.

FILET CROCHET

Follow the chart. An open square = 1 dc, ch 2, skip 2 sts of previous row, 1 dc. A filled square = 4 dc. On the chart, the last st of 1 square serves as the first st of the foll square.

DIRECTIONS

Along each edge of handkerchief, work 198 sc with 3 sc in each corner. (Insert hook directly into the handkerchief 1 or 2 threads from the edge.) You now have 201 sts on each side. Join round with 1 sl st. Continue by foll the chart. On each corner center st, work increases by foll corner chart (shown on page 52) for the first 3 rounds, then on rem rounds, work same as round 2 when working on a filled square and same as round 3 on last 2 rounds. For filet pattern, work pat chart between arrows 2 and 3, then work between arrows 1 and 2 twice on each side. Beg each round with ch 3 and end each round by working 1 sl st in the 3rd ch of the turning ch of the previous round. Work the 10 rounds of pat chart. Fasten off.

FINISHING

Pin piece to indicated measurement, pinning many times along each edge. Dampen and let dry.

HANDKERCHIEF EDGING
See photo on page 32 B

SIZE

Approx. 1¹/³" wide.

MATERIALS

15 g crochet cotton thread. Steel crochet hook U.S. size 14. (U.K. size 6) 1 handkerchief 9¾" x 9¾".

STITCHES USED

U.S. - Chain stitch (ch), slip stitch (sl st), single crochet (sc), double crochet (dc). U.K. - chain stitch, slip stitch, double crochet, treble crochet.

GAUGE

14 squares x 14 rows = 4" x 4".

FILET CROCHET

Follow the chart. An open square = 1 dc, ch 2, skip 2 sts of previous row, 1 dc. A filled square = 4 dc. On the chart, the last st of 1 square serves as the first st of the foll square.

DIRECTIONS

Along each edge of handkerchief, work 195 sc with 3 sc in each corner. (Insert hook directly into the handkerchief 1 or 2 threads from the edge.) You now have 198 sts on each side. Follow chart: Beg round 1, 9 sc from 1 corner. Work from point 2 to 3 for corner, then work from point 1 to 2, 6 times for each side. Join rounds with 1 sl st. Continue by foll the chart. Beg each round with ch 3 and end each round by working 1 sl st in the 3rd ch of the turning ch of the previous round. Work the 10 rounds of pat chart. In the point of each corner center st, work increases by foll corner chart (shown on page 52). Work same as round 2 of corner chart when working on a filled square and same as round 3 of corner chart when working on an open square. Fasten off.

FINISHING

Pin piece to indicated measurement, pinning many times along each edge. Dampen and let dry.

HANDKERCHIEF EDGING
See photo on page 32 C

SIZE

Approx. 1¾" wide.

MATERIALS

15 g crochet cotton thread. Steel crochet hook U.S. size 14. (U.K. size 6) 1 handkerchief 9¾" x 9¾".

STITCHES USED

U.S. - Chain stitch (ch), slip stitch (sl st), single crochet (sc), double crochet (dc). U.K. - chain stitch, slip stitch, double crochet, treble crochet.

GAUGE

14 squares x 14 rows = 4" x 4".

FILET CROCHET

Follow the chart. An open square = 1 dc, ch 2, skip 2 sts of previous row, 1 dc. A filled square = 4 dc. On the chart, the last st of 1 square serves as the first st of the foll square.

DIRECTIONS

Along each edge of handkerchief, work 198 sc with 3 sc in each corner. (Insert hook directly into the handkerchief 1 or 2 threads from the edge.) You now have 201 sts on each side. Beg round 1 of chart 33 sts from 1 corner and work from point 2 to 3 for corner, work from point 1 to 2, 3 times total for each side, work all around, following chart. Beg each round with ch 3 and end each round by working 1 sl st in the 3rd ch of the turning ch of the previous round. Work the 15 rounds of pat chart. In the point of each corner center st, work increases by foll corner chart (shown on page 52). Work same as round 2 when working on a filled square and same as round 3 when working on an open square. Fasten off.

FINISHING

Pin piece to indicated measurement, pinning many times along each edge. Dampen and let dry.

HANDKERCHIEF EDGING
See photo on page 32 D

SIZE

Approx. 1½" wide.

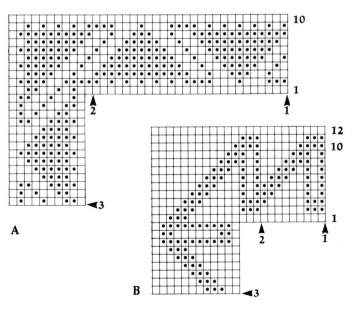

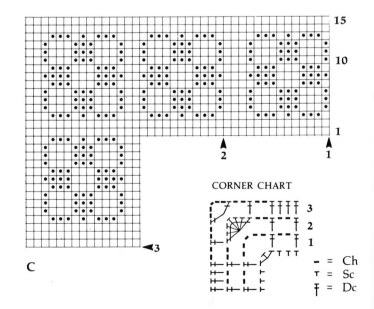

MATERIALS

15 g crochet cotton thread. Steel crochet hook U.S. size 14. (U.K. size 6) 1 handkerchief 9¾" x 9¾".

STITCHES USED

U.S. - Chain stitch (ch), slip stitch (sl st), single crochet (sc), double crochet (dc). U.K. - chain stitch, slip stitch, double crochet, treble crochet.

GAUGE

14 squares x 14 rows = 4" x 4".

FILET CROCHET

Follow the chart. An open square = 1 dc, ch 2, skip 2 sts of previous row, 1 dc. A filled square = 4 dc. On the chart, the last st of 1 square serves as the first st of the foll square.

DIRECTIONS

Along each edge of handkerchief, work 201 sc with 3 sc in each corner. (Insert hook directly into the handkerchief 1 or 2 threads from the edge.) You now have 204 sts on each side. Follow chart: Beg round 1, 6 sts from 1 corner. For each corner, work from double arrow to double arrow on chart. For each side, work from single arrow to single arrow 5 times. Work all around, following chart. Beg each round with ch 3 and end each round by working 1 sl st in the 3rd ch of the turning ch of the previous round. Work the 14 rounds of pat chart. In the point of each corner center st, work increases by foll corner chart (shown on page 53). Work same as round 2 when working on a filled square and same as round 3 when working on an open square. Fasten off.

FINISHING

Pin piece to indicated measurement, pinning many times along each edge. Dampen and let dry.

HANDKERCHIEF EDGING
See photo on page 32 E

SIZE

Approx. 1½" wide.

MATERIALS

15 g crochet cotton thread. Steel crochet hook U.S. size 14. (U.K. size 6) 1 handkerchief 9¾" x 9¾".

STITCHES USED

U.S. - Chain stitch (ch), slip stitch (sl st), single crochet (sc), double crochet (dc). U.K. - chain stitch, slip stitch, double crochet, treble crochet.

GAUGE

14 squares x 14 rows = 4" x 4".

FILET CROCHET

Follow the chart. An open square = 1 dc, ch 2, skip 2 sts of previous row, 1 dc. A filled square = 4 dc. On the chart, the last st of 1 square serves as the first st of the foll square.

DIRECTIONS

Along each edge of handkerchief, work 198 sc with 3 sc in each corner. (Insert hook directly into the handkerchief 1 or 2 threads from the edge.) You now have 201 sts on each side. Follow chart: Beg round 1, 6 sts from 1 corner. For each corner, work from point 2 to point 3 on chart. For each side, work from point 1

and 2, 4 times. Work all around, following chart. Beg each round with ch 3 and end each round by working 1 sl st in the 3rd ch of the turning ch of the previous round. Work the 13 rounds of pat chart. In the point of each center corner st, work increases by foll corner chart (shown on page 52). Work same as round 2 when working on a filled square and same as round 3 when working on an open square. Fasten off.

FINISHING

Pin piece to indicated measurement, pinning many times along each edge. Dampen and let dry.

HANDKERCHIEF EDGING
See photo on page 34 A

SIZE

Handkerchief approx. 9¾" x 9¾" + edging.

MATERIALS

10 g white crochet cotton thread. Steel crochet hook U.S. size 14. (U.K. size 6) 1 handkerchief 9¾" x 9¾".

NOTE: The handkerchief with edging is dyed after it is completed.

STITCHES USED

U.S. - Chain stitch (ch), slip stitch (sl st), single crochet (sc), double crochet (dc), picot. U.K. - chain stitch, slip stitch, double crochet, treble crochet, picot.

FILET CROCHET

Follow the chart. An open square = 1 dc, ch 2, skip 2 sts of previous row, 1 dc. A filled square = 4 dc. On the chart, the last st of 1 square serves as the first st of the foll square.

DIRECTIONS

Along each edge of handkerchief, work 198 sc with 3 sc in each corner. (Insert hook directly into the handkerchief 1 or 2 threads from the edge.) You now have 201 sts along each edge. Join round with 1 sl st. Beg first round of chart 27 sts from 1 corner st. For each corner, work between arrows 2 through 3. For the even edges, work between arrows 1 to 2 twice. Beg each round with ch 3 and join each round with a sl st in the 3rd ch of the turning ch of previous round. Continue by foll the chart. On each center corner st, work increases by foll corner chart for the first 3 rounds, then on rem rounds, work same as round 2 when working on a filled square and same as round 3 on last 2 rounds. Work

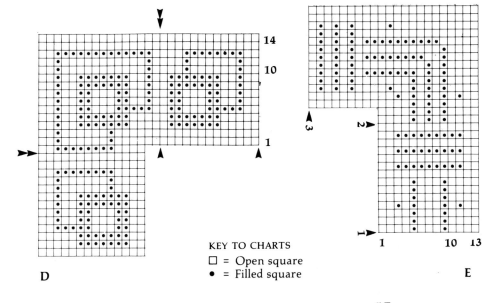

KEY TO CHARTS
☐ = Open square
● = Filled square

D

E

the 10 rounds of pat chart. Fasten off. Work picots by foll chart: Join thread to edge, *ch 5 and sl st to first ch, sl st across 5 squares*, rep * to * around. Fasten off.

FINISHING

Dye finished piece to desired color. Pin piece to indicated measurement, pinning at each picot. Dampen and let dry.

HANDKERCHIEF EDGING

See photo on page 34 B

SIZE

Handkerchief approx. 9¾" x 9¾" + edging.

MATERIALS

15 g white crochet cotton thread. Steel crochet hook U.S. size 14. (U.K. size 6) 1 handkerchief 9¾" x 9¾".

NOTE: The handkerchief with edging is dyed after it is completed.

STITCHES USED

U.S. - Chain stitch (ch), slip stitch (sl st), single crochet (sc), double crochet (dc). U.K. - chain stitch, slip stitch, double crochet, treble crochet.

FILET CROCHET

Follow the chart. An open square = 1 dc, ch 2, skip 2 sts of previous row, 1 dc. A filled square = 4 dc. On the chart, the last st of 1 square serves as the first st of the foll square.

DIRECTIONS

Along each edge of handkerchief, work 198 sc with 3 sc in each corner. (Insert hook directly into the handkerchief 1 or 2 threads from the edge.) You now have 201 sts along each edge. Join round with 1 sl st. Beg first round of chart 15 sts from 1 corner st. For each corner, work between arrows 2 through 3. For the even edges, work between arrows 1 to 2 once. Beg each round with ch 3 and join each round with a sl st in the 3rd ch of the turning ch of previous round. Continue by foll the chart. On each center corner st, work increases by foll corner chart for the first 3 rounds, then on rem rounds, work same as round 2 when working on a filled square and same as round 3 on last 2 rounds. Work the 15 rounds of pat chart. Fasten off.

FINISHING

Dye finished piece to desired color. Pin piece to indicated measurement. Dampen and let dry.

HANDKERCHIEF EDGING

See photo on page 34 C

SIZE

Handkerchief approx. 9¾" x 9¾" + edging.

MATERIALS

10 g white crochet cotton thread. Steel crochet hook U.S. size 14. (U.K. size 6) 1 handkerchief 9¾" x 9¾".

NOTE: The handkerchief with edging is dyed after it is completed.

STITCHES USED

U.S. - Chain stitch (ch), slip stitch (sl st), single crochet (sc), double crochet (dc). U.K. - chain stitch, slip stitch, double crochet, treble crochet.

FILET CROCHET

Follow the chart. An open square = 1 dc, ch 2, skip 2 sts of previous row, 1 dc. A filled square = 4 dc. On the chart, the last st of 1 square serves as the first st of the foll square.

DIRECTIONS

Along each edge of handkerchief, work 198 sc with 3 sc in each corner. (Insert hook directly into the handkerchief 1 or 2 threads from the edge.) You now have 201 sts along each edge. Join round with 1 sl st. Beg first round of chart 21 sts from 1 corner st. For each corner, work between arrows 2 through 3. For the even edges, work between arrows 1 to 2 once. Beg each round with ch 3 and join each round with a sl st in the 3rd ch of the turning ch of previous round. Continue by foll the chart. On each center corner st, work increases by foll corner chart for the first 3 rounds, then on rem rounds, work same as round 2

when working on a filled square and same as round 3 on last 2 rounds. Work the 12 rounds of pat chart. Fasten off.

FINISHING

Dye finished piece to desired color. Pin piece to indicated measurement. Dampen and let dry.

HANDKERCHIEF EDGING

See photo on page 34 D

SIZE

Handkerchief approx. 9¾" x 9¾" + edging.

MATERIALS

15 g white crochet cotton thread. Steel crochet hook U.S. size 14. (U.K. size 6) 1 handkerchief 9¾" x 9¾".

NOTE: The handkerchief with edging is dyed after it is completed.

STITCHES USED

U.S. - Chain stitch (ch), slip stitch (sl st), single crochet (sc), double crochet (dc). U.K. - chain stitch, slip stitch, double crochet, treble crochet.

FILET CROCHET

Follow the chart. An open square = 1 dc, ch 2, skip 2 sts of previous row, 1 dc. A filled square = 4 dc. On the chart, the last st of 1 square serves as the first st of the foll square.

DIRECTIONS

Along each edge of handkerchief, work 198 sc with 3 sc in each corner. (Insert hook directly into the handkerchief 1 or 2 threads from the edge.) You now have 201 sts along each edge. Join round with 1 sl st. Beg first round of chart 15 sts

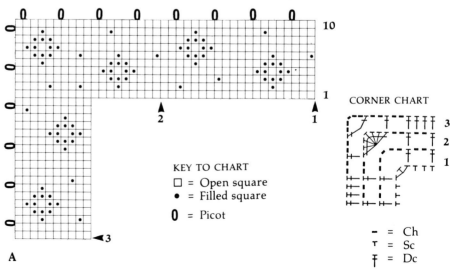

KEY TO CHART

□ = Open square
• = Filled square
0 = Picot

CORNER CHART

− = Ch
τ = Sc
† = Dc

A

54

from 1 corner st. For each corner, work between arrows 2 through 3. For the even edges, work between arrows 1 to 2 once. Beg each round with ch 3 and join each round with a sl st in the 3rd ch of the turning ch of previous round. Continue by foll the chart. For corners, follow the chart: on each center corner st, work same as round 2 when working on a filled square and same as round 3 on an open square. Fasten off.

FINISHING
Dye finished piece to desired color. Pin piece to indicated measurement. Dampen and let dry.

HANDKERCHIEF EDGING
See photo on page 34 E

SIZE
Handkerchief approx. 9¾″ x 9¾″ + edging.

MATERIALS
15 g white crochet cotton thread. Steel

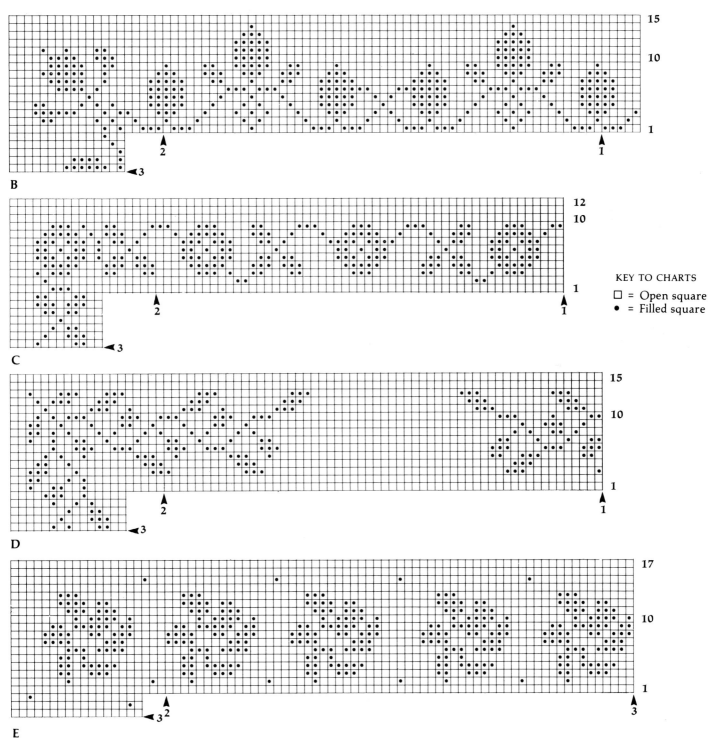

KEY TO CHARTS

☐ = Open square
● = Filled square

crochet hook U.S. size 14. (U.K. size 6) 1 handkerchief 9¾" x 9¾".

NOTE: The handkerchief with edging is dyed after it is completed.

STITCHES USED
U.S. - Chain stitch (ch), slip stitch (sl st), single crochet (sc), double crochet (dc). U.K. - chain stitch, slip stitch, double crochet, treble crochet.

FILET CROCHET
Follow the chart. An open square = 1 dc, ch 2, skip 2 sts of previous row, 1 dc. A filled square = 4 dc. On the chart, the last st of 1 square serves as the first st of the foll square.

DIRECTIONS
Along each edge of handkerchief, work 198 sc with 3 sc in each corner. (Insert hook directly into the handkerchief 1 or 2 threads from the edge.) You now have 201 sts along each edge. Join round with 1 sl st. Beg first round of chart 9 sts from 1 corner st. For each corner, work between arrows 2 through 3. For the even edges, work between arrows 1 to 2 once. Beg each round with ch 3 and join each round with a sl st in the 3rd ch of the turning ch of previous round. Continue by foll the chart. For corners, follow the chart: on each center corner st, work same as round 2 when working

on a filled square and same as round 3 on an open square. Complete 17 rounds of chart. Fasten off.

FINISHING
Dye finished piece to desired color. Pin piece to indicated measurement. Dampen and let dry.

HANDKERCHIEF EDGING
See photo on page 36

SIZE
Approx. 11¾" x 11¾". Width of the point about 1".

MATERIALS
10 g fine crochet cotton thread. Steel crochet hook U.S. size 14. (U.K. size 6) 10½" x 10½" fine cotton fabric.

STITCHES USED
U.S. - Chain stitch (ch), slip stitch (sl st), single crochet (sc), double crochet (dc), triple crochet (tr). U.K. - chain stitch, slip stitch, double crochet, treble crochet, double treble crochet.

GAUGE
29½ squares in height and width = 4" x 4".

FILET CROCHET
Follow the chart. An open square = 1 dc,

ch 2, skip 2 sts of previous row, 1 dc. A filled square = 4 dc. On the chart, the last st of 1 square serves as the first st of the foll square.

DIRECTIONS
Pull out a thread ⅛" from each edge of fabric. Roll the edge to wrong side and work 222 sc along each edge by inserting hook in the open row and working 3 sc in each corner, sl st to join.
ROUND 1: Ch 5, skip 2 sc, *1 dc, ch 2, skip 2 sc of the previous row*, rep * to * to corner, work 1 dc, ch 5 in each corner st. Continue around sl st to join in the 3rd ch of the previous round.
ROUNDS 2 to 5: Continue by foll chart, working 2nd half to correspond. To work corners, see detailed chart. Beg each round with ch 3. Finish with 1 row of sc by working 1 sc in each dc and 2 sc in each ch arc. Fasten off.

FINISHING
Pin piece to indicated measurement. Dampen and let dry.

HANDKERCHIEF EDGING
See photo on page 37

SIZE
Approx. 12¼" x 12¼". Width of the point about 1⅛".

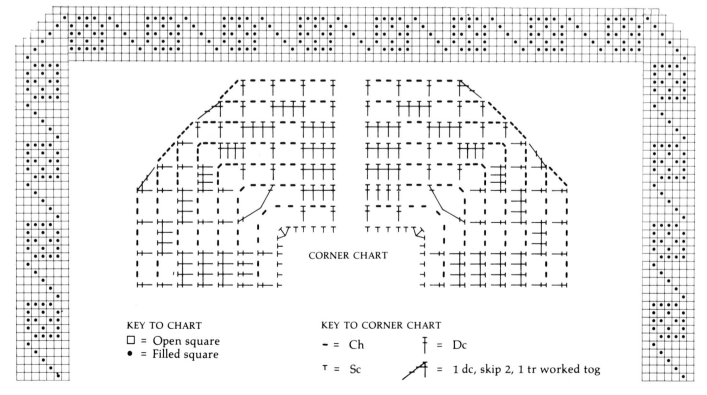

CORNER CHART

KEY TO CHART
☐ = Open square
● = Filled square

KEY TO CORNER CHART

- = Ch   † = Dc

ᴛ = Sc   ⟋Ⱶ = 1 dc, skip 2, 1 tr worked tog

MATERIALS

10 g fine crochet cotton thread. Steel crochet hook U.S. size 14. (U.K. size 6) 8½" x 8½" fine cotton fabric.

STITCHES USED

U.S. - Chain stitch (ch), slip stitch (sl st), single crochet (sc), double crochet (dc). U.K. - chain stitch, slip stitch, double crochet, treble crochet.

GAUGE

29½ squares in height and width = 4" x 4".

FILET CROCHET

Follow the chart. An open square = 1 dc, ch 2, skip 2 sts of previous row, 1 dc. A filled square = 4 dc. On the chart, the last st of 1 square serves as the first st of the foll square.

DIRECTIONS

Pull out a thread ⅛" from each edge of fabric. Roll the edge to wrong side and work 174 sc along each edge by inserting hook in the open row and working 3 sc in each corner, sl st to join. ROUND 1: Ch 5, skip 2 sc, *1 dc, ch 2, skip 2 sc of the previous row*, rep * to * to corner, work 1 dc, ch 5 in each corner st. Continue around sl st to join in the 3rd ch of the previous round.
ROUNDS 2 to 15: Continue by foll chart. In the first dc of each round, ch 3 and

join each round with 1 sl st in the 3rd ch of the previous round. For the corner inc in an open square, work 1 dc, ch 5. For a corner inc in a filled square, work 6 dc in the center dc of the previous round. Beg each round with ch 3. Fasten off.

FINISHING

Pin piece to indicated measurement. Dampen and let dry.

EDGING

See photo on page 38 A

SIZE

Approx. 4¼" wide. Each pat repeat is about 1¾" long.

MATERIALS

For each 45¼", 50 g crochet cotton thread. Steel crochet hook U.S. size 10. (U.K. size 4)

STITCHES USED

U.S. - Chain stitch (ch), double crochet (dc). U.K. - chain stitch, treble crochet.

GAUGE

21 squares = 4¼" wide. 10 rows = 1¾" long.

FILET CROCHET

Follow the chart. An open square = 1 dc, ch 2, skip 2 sts of previous row, 1 dc. A filled square = 3 dc. On the chart, the

last st of 1 square serves as the first st of the foll square.

DIRECTIONS

Ch 63 + ch 3 to turn (serves as first dc). ROW 1: 1 dc in the 4th, 5th, and 6th ch from the hook (= 1 filled square), continue by foll chart = 21 squares. Continue by foll chart from rows 2 to 10, then work rows 1 to 10 until desired length. Beg each row without incs or decs with ch 3 to turn, work last dc in 3rd ch of turning ch of previous row. Work inc and dec as shown on chart. Fasten off.

FINISHING

Pin piece to indicated measurement. Dampen and let dry.

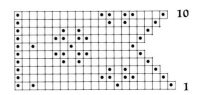

KEY TO CHART

☐ = Open square
● = Filled square

EDGING

See photo on page 38 B

SIZE

Approx. 4¼" wide. Each pat repeat is about 1¾" long.

MATERIALS

For each 43¼", 50 g crochet cotton thread. Steel crochet hook U.S. size 10. (U.K. size 4)

STITCHES USED

U.S. - Chain stitch (ch), double crochet (dc). U.K. - chain stitch, treble crochet.

GAUGE

21 squares = 4¼" wide. 10 rows = 1¾" long.

FILET CROCHET

Follow the chart. An open square = 1 dc, ch 2, skip 2 sts of previous row, 1 dc. A filled square = 3 dc. On the chart, the last st of 1 square serves as the first st of the foll square.

DIRECTIONS

Ch 63 + ch 3 to turn (serves as first dc). ROW 1: 1 dc in the 4th, 5th, and 6th ch from the hook(= 1 filled square), continue by foll chart = 21 squares.

KEY TO CHART

☐ = Open square
●· = Filled square

Continue by foll chart from rows 2 to 10, then work rows 1 to 10 until desired length. Beg each row with ch 3 to turn, work last dc in 3rd ch of turning ch of previous row. Fasten off.

FINISHING

Pin piece to indicated measurement. Dampen and let dry.

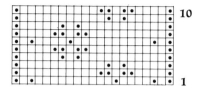

10

1

KEY TO CHART
□ = Open square
● = Filled square

EDGING
See photo on page 38 C

SIZE
Approx. 5¼" wide. Each pat repeat is about 1" long.

MATERIALS
For each 31½", 50 g crochet cotton thread. Steel crochet hook U.S. size 10. (U.K. size 4)

STITCHES USED
U.S. - Chain stitch (ch), double crochet (dc). U.K. - chain stitch, treble crochet.

GAUGE
24 squares = 5¼" wide. 6 rows = 1" long.

FILET CROCHET
Follow the chart. An open square = 1 dc, ch 2, skip 2 sts of previous row, 1 dc. A filled square = 3 dc. On the chart, the last st of 1 square serves as the first st of the foll square.

6

1

KEY TO CHART
□ = Open square
● = Filled square

DIRECTIONS
Ch 72 + ch 3 to turn (serves as first dc).
ROW 1: 1 dc in the 4th, 5th, and 6th ch from the hook(= 1 filled square), continue by foll chart = 24 squares.

Continue by foll chart from rows 2 to 6, then work rows 1 to 6 until desired length. Beg each row with ch 3 to turn, work last dc in 3rd ch of turning ch of previous row. Fasten off.

FINISHING

Pin piece to indicated measurement. Dampen and let dry.

EDGING
See photo on page 38 D

SIZE
Approx. 4¾" wide. Each pat repeat is about 1¹/₃" long.

MATERIALS
For each 35½", 50 g crochet cotton thread. Steel crochet hook U.S. size 10. (U.K. size 4)

STITCHES USED
U.S. - Chain stitch (ch), double crochet (dc). U.K. - chain stitch, treble crochet.

GAUGE
23 squares = 4¾" wide. 8 rows = 1¹/₃" long.

FILET CROCHET
Follow the chart. An open square = 1 dc, ch 2, skip 2 sts of previous row, 1 dc. A filled square = 3 dc. On the chart, the last st of 1 square serves as the first st of the foll square.

DIRECTIONS
Ch 74.
ROW 1: 1 dc in the 8th ch from the hook, (= 1 open square), continue by foll the chart = 23 squares. Continue by foll chart from rows 2 to 8, then work rows 1 to 8 until desired length. Beg each row with ch 3 to turn, work last dc in 3rd ch of turning ch of previous row. Fasten off.

FINISHING

Pin piece to indicated measurement. Dampen and let dry.

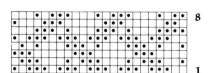

8

1

KEY TO CHART
□ = Open square
● = Filled square

EDGING
See photo on page 38 E

SIZE
Approx. 4¼" wide. Each pat repeat is about 1¾" long.

MATERIALS
For each 39¼", 50 g crochet cotton thread. Steel crochet hook U.S. size 10. (U.K. size 4)

STITCHES USED
U.S. - Chain stitch (ch), double crochet (dc). U.K. - chain stitch, treble crochet.

GAUGE
20 squares = 4¼" wide. 10 rows = 1¾" long.

FILET CROCHET
Follow the chart. An open square = 1 dc, ch 2, skip 2 sts of previous row, 1 dc. A filled square = 3 dc. On the chart, the last st of 1 square serves as the first st of the foll square.

DIRECTIONS
Ch 65.
ROW 1: 1 dc in the 8th ch from the hook, (= 1 open square), continue by foll the chart = 20 squares. Continue by foll chart from rows 2 to 10, then work rows 1 to 10 until desired length. Beg each row with ch 3 to turn, work last dc in 3rd ch of turning ch of previous row. Fasten off.

FINISHING

Pin piece to indicated measurement. Dampen and let dry.

10

1

KEY TO CHART
□ = Open square
● = Filled square

EDGING
See photo on page 38 F

SIZE
Approx. 4¾" wide. Each pat repeat is about 4" long.

MATERIALS
For each 35½", 50 g crochet cotton

thread. Steel crochet hook U.S. size 10. (U.K. size 4)

STITCHES USED
U.S. - Chain stitch (ch), double crochet (dc). U.K. - chain stitch, treble crochet.

GAUGE
23 squares = 4¾" wide. 10 rows = 4" long.

FILET CROCHET
Follow the chart. An open square = 1 dc, ch 2, skip 2 sts of previous row, 1 dc. A filled square = 3 dc. On the chart, the last st of 1 square serves as the first st of the foll square.

DIRECTIONS
Ch 74.
ROW 1: 1 dc in the 8th ch from the hook, (= 1 open square), continue by foll the chart = 23 squares. Continue by foll chart from rows 2 to 24, then work rows 1 to 24 until desired length. Beg each row with ch 3 to turn, work last dc in 3rd ch of turning ch of previous row. Fasten off.

FINISHING
Pin piece to indicated measurement. Dampen and let dry.

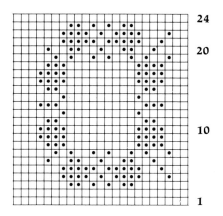

KEY TO CHART
□ = Open square
● = Filled square

EDGING
See photo on page 38 G
SIZE
Approx. 4¼" wide. Each pat repeat is about 7" long.

MATERIALS
For each 47¼", 50 g crochet cotton

thread. Steel crochet hook U.S. size 10. (U.K. size 4)

STITCHES USED
U.S. - Chain stitch (ch), double crochet (dc). U.K. - chain stitch, treble crochet.

GAUGE
20 squares = 4¼" wide. 40 rows = 7" long.

FILET CROCHET
Follow the chart. An open square = 1 dc, ch 2, skip 2 sts of previous row, 1 dc. A filled square = 3 dc. On the chart, the last st of 1 square serves as the first st of the foll square.

DIRECTIONS
Ch 60 + ch 3 to turn (serves as first dc).
ROW 1: 1 dc in the 4th, 5th, 6th, 7th, 8th, and 9th ch from the hook, (= 2 filled squares), continue by foll the chart = 20 squares. Continue by foll chart from rows 2 to 40, then work rows 1 to 40 until desired length. Beg each row with ch 3 to turn, work last dc in 3rd ch of turning ch of previous row. Fasten off.

FINISHING
Pin piece to indicated measurement. Dampen and let dry.

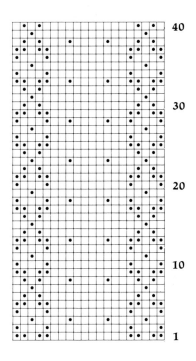

KEY TO CHART
□ = Open square
● = Filled square

EDGING
See photo on page 38 H
SIZE
Approx. 4¼" wide. Each pat repeat is about 7" long.

MATERIALS
For each 51¼", 50 g crochet cotton thread. Steel crochet hook U.S. size 10. (U.K. size 4)

STITCHES USED
U.S. - Chain stitch (ch), double crochet (dc). U.K. - chain stitch, treble crochet.

GAUGE
17 squares = 4¼" wide. 40 rows = 7" long.

FILET CROCHET
Follow the chart. An open square = 1 dc, ch 2, skip 2 sts of previous row, 1 dc. A filled square = 3 dc. On the chart, the last st of 1 square serves as the first st of the foll square.

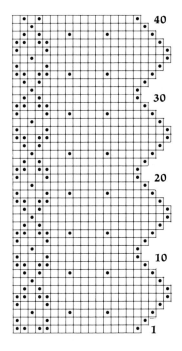

KEY TO CHART
□ = Open square
● = Filled square

DIRECTIONS
Ch 51 + ch 3 to turn (serves as first dc).
ROW 1: 1 dc in the 4th, 5th, and 6th ch from the hook, (= 1 filled square), continue by foll the chart = 17 squares. Continue by foll chart from rows 2 to

40, then work rows 1 to 40 until desired length. Work inc and dec as shown on chart. Beg each row without incs or decs with ch 3 to turn, work last dc in 3rd ch of turning ch of previous row. Fasten off.

FINISHING

Pin piece to indicated measurement. Dampen and let dry.

LINGERIE BAG
See photo on page 38 I

SIZE

Approx. 4¾" wide. Each pat repeat is about 3½" long. Bag size: approx. 11" x 11".

MATERIALS

50 g crochet cotton thread. Steel crochet hook U.S. size 10. (U.K. size 4) 19¾" x 51¼" white cotton. 31½" x ¾" white ribbon.

STITCHES USED

U.S. - Chain stitch (ch), double crochet (dc). U.K. - chain stitch, treble crochet.

FILET CROCHET

Follow the chart. An open square = 1 dc, ch 2, skip 2 sts of previous row, 1 dc. A filled square = 3 dc. On the chart, the last st of 1 square serves as the first st of the foll square.

GAUGE

22 squares = 4¾" wide. 20 rows = 3½" long.

DIRECTIONS

Ch 66 + ch 3 to turn (serves as first dc). ROW 1: 1 dc in the 4th, 5th, and 6th ch from the hook (= 1 filled square), continue by foll chart = 22 squares. Continue by foll chart from rows 2 to 20, then work rows 1 to 20 twice. Work inc and dec as shown on chart. Beg each row without incs or decs with ch 3 to turn, work last dc in 3rd ch of turning ch of previous row. Fasten off.

FINISHING

Pin piece to indicated measurement. Dampen and let dry. Cut a piece of fabric 51¼" x 11¾" and 2nd piece of cotton 8" x 16½". Fold the smaller piece by foll diagram. Mark the pleats and iron ¼" pleats, opening to the outside. When pleated, the piece will measure 8" x 11¾". Sew the 11¾" ends of the small

piece to the narrow ends of first piece of fabric to form a ring. Fold the piece at 1 seam, wrong sides together. (Juncture of pleated piece and plain piece. This end will be the lower edge.) Fold in all edges by ¼" and iron seams. Sew side seams through all thicknesses. Fold the plain piece so that folded end meets the inside seam of the pleated part and sew side seams of the pocket which has been formed. Baste the crocheted edging to right side of lower edge of pocket flap. Sew on the ribbon along the side seams and the lower edge of pocket flap, making mitered corner.

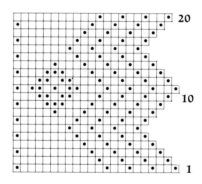

KEY TO CHART

□ = Open square
● = Filled square

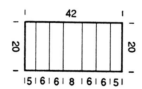

SKIRT EDGING
See photo on pages 40 - 41

SIZE

Approx. 4¾" x 98½".

MATERIALS

100 g crochet cotton thread. Steel crochet hook U.S. size 10. (U.K. size 4)

STITCHES USED

U.S. - Chain stitch (ch), double crochet (dc). U.K. - chain stitch, treble crochet.

GAUGE

10 squares in height and 9 squares in width = 2" x 2".

FILET CROCHET

Follow the chart. An open square = 1 dc,

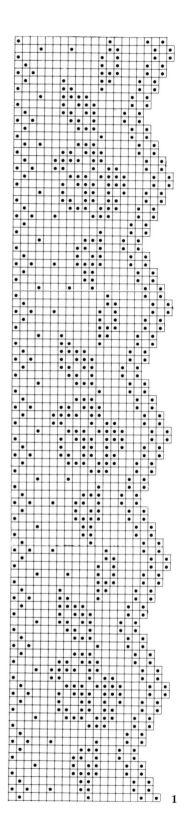

KEY TO CHART

□ = Open square
● = Filled square

ch 2, skip 2 sts of previous row, 1 dc. A filled square = 4 dc. On the chart, the last st of 1 square serves as the first st of the foll square. To dec a square at the end of row: leave last square unworked. To inc a filled square at end of row: Ch 6, (= ch 3 for new square + ch 3 for first dc) 1 dc in 5th ch from hook, 1 dc in foll st.

DIRECTIONS

Ch 61 + ch 3 to turn (serves as first dc).
ROW 1: 1 dc in the 5th, 6th and 7th ch from the hook, *ch 2, skip 2 ch, 1 dc* (= 1 open square), 1 dc in each of the foll 3 dc (= 1 filled square), work * to * 6 times, 1 filled square, 8 open squares, 1 filled square, end with 1 open square.
ROW 2: Ch 3, 1 filled square above 1 open square (= 2 dc in the ch 2, 1 dc in the foll dc), 1 open square (= ch 2, skip 2, 1 dc in the foll dc), 1 filled square, 2 open squares, 1 filled square, 3 open squares, 1 filled square above 1 open square, 1 filled square above a filled square (= 1 dc in the foll 3 dc), 5 open squares, 1 filled square, 1 open square, 1 filled square, leave the last square unworked. Continue by foll chart, rep chart until piece measures 98½" or desired length, ending with row 1. Beg each row without incs or decs with ch 3 and on rows which end without inc or dec, work the last dc in the 3rd ch of the turning ch of the previous row. Fasten off.

FINISHING

Pin piece to indicated measurement. Dampen and let dry. Sew first row to last row of piece and sew to lower edge of a skirt.

TOWEL EDGING

See photo on page 42, top

For Shelf Edging, see photo on page 27

SIZE

Border approx. 5" wide. 1 rep = 4".

MATERIALS

50 g crochet cotton thread. Steel crochet hook U.S. size 7. (U.K. size 2.5) Terry cloth fabric approx. 19¾" x 39¼".

STITCHES USED

U.S. - Chain stitch (ch), double crochet (dc). U.K. - chain stitch, treble crochet.

GAUGE

14 squares x 16 rows = 4" x 4".

FILET CROCHET

Follow the chart. An open square = 1 dc, ch 2, skip 2 sts of previous row, 1 dc. A filled square = 4 dc. On the chart, the last st of 1 square serves as the first st of the foll square.

DIRECTIONS

Ch 42 + ch 3 to turn (serves as first dc).
ROW 1: 1 dc in the 4th ch from the hook, 1 dc in each of the foll ch = 43 dc. Continue by foll chart from rows 2 to 16, then work rows 17 to 32 to desired length, end with rows 33 to 49. Beg each row without incs or decs with ch 3 and always work the last dc in the 3rd ch of the turning ch of previous row. Fasten off.

FINISHING

Pin piece to indicated measurement (19¾" x 5"). Dampen and let dry. Make hems along all edges of fabric. Sew on border along lower edge of fabric over hem.

See chart on page 48, top left.

TOWEL EDGING

See photo on page 42, bottom

SIZE

Towel size approx. 20½" x 40½". Border approx. 4¼" wide.

MATERIALS

50 g crochet cotton thread. Steel crochet hook U.S. size 6. (U.K. size 2) Blue and white tweed terry cloth material 37¼" long x 21¼" wide. For a hanger, cotton binding about 4¾" long.

STITCHES USED

U.S. - Chain stitch (ch), slip stitch (sl st), double crochet (dc). U.K. - chain stitch, slip stitch, treble crochet.

GAUGE

8 squares in height and width = 4" x 4".

FILET CROCHET

Follow the chart. An open square = 1 dc, ch 2, skip 2 sts of previous row, 1 dc. A filled square = 4 dc. On the chart, the last st of 1 square serves as the first st of the foll square.

DIRECTIONS

Ch 207 + ch 3 to turn (serves as first dc).
ROW 1: 1 dc in the 4th ch from the hook and 1 dc in each ch across = 208 dc.
ROWS 2 to 9: Foll the chart, beg each row with ch 3. Work the last dc in the 3rd ch at beg of previous row.
ROW 10: Sl st over first square, ch 3 and work across chart for 11 squares. Turn.
ROW 11 to 14: Sl st over first square, work as shown on chart, leave last square unworked. Turn. After row 14, fasten off. Rejoin yarn 3 squares from first point and work in the same way until all points are complete.

FINISHING

Pin piece to indicated measurement. Dampen and let dry. Zigzag stitch along all edges of terry cloth, then make a ¼" hem. Fold cotton binding in half and place in the hem at top edge. Sew hems in place. Place the crochet border on the right side of the towel and sew in place.

KEY TO CHART

□ = Open square
• = Filled square

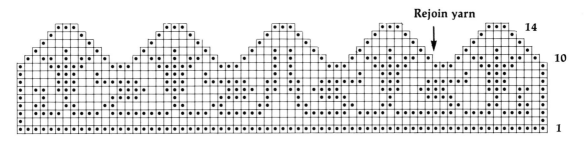

TOWEL EDGING
See photo on page 43

SIZE
Towels: 19¾" x 39¼" long. Width of inserts: 2½". Width of edging: 3 1/3".

MATERIALS
50 g gold crochet cotton thread. Steel crochet hook U.S. size 6. (U.K. size 2) Gold and white striped towel 19¾" x 39¼".

STITCHES USED
U.S. - Chain stitch (ch), slip stitch (sl st), double crochet (dc). U.K. - chain stitch, slip stitch, treble crochet.

GAUGE
6 squares x 7 rows = 2" x 2".

FILET CROCHET
Follow the chart. An open square = 1 dc, ch 2, skip 2 sts of previous row, 1 dc. A filled square = 4 dc. On the chart, the last st of 1 square serves as the first st of the foll square.

DIRECTIONS
INSERT
Ch 18 + ch 3 to turn.
ROW 1: 1 dc in the 4th ch from the hook, 1 dc in each of the foll 8 ch, *ch 2, skip 2, 1 dc*, work * to * 3 times total. Work by foll chart, rep rows 2 to 7, beg each row with ch 3. Work last dc in the 3rd st of the ch 3 at beg of previous row. Rep rows between the arrows 10 times, then work 1 row of sc along straight edges as foll: work 2 sc in the ch arc between the dc and 1 sc in every dc and 1 sc in each corner. Ch 3 to turn, then work 1 dc in each sc of previous row. Fasten off.

EDGING
Work same as above by foll chart and increasing and decreasing as indicated on chart.

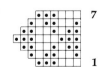

KEY TO CHART
☐ = Open square
● = Filled square

FINISHING
Pin piece to indicated measurement. Dampen and let dry. Cut a 2½" strip from the lower edge of the towel and zigzag stitch the edges, turning under ⅛" on edge of towel and long edges on stripe. Place the insert and edging on right side of towel and strip to cover the hem and sew in place.

CURTAIN
See photo on page 44

SIZE
Curtain: approx. 31½" x 44½". Vertical Inserts: 4" wide. Edging: 5" wide.

MATERIALS
200 g crochet cotton. Steel crochet hook U.S. size 4. (U.K. size 1) Cotton fabric about 48" long and 35½" wide. White sewing thread and 1 wooden dowel about 32" long.

STITCHES USED
U.S. - Chain stitch (ch), double crochet (dc). U.K. - chain stitch, treble crochet.

GAUGE
13 squares x 16 rows = 4" x 4".

FILET CROCHET
Follow the chart. An open square = 1 dc, ch 2, skip 2 sts of previous row, 1 dc. A filled square = 4 dc. On the chart, the last st of 1 square serves as the first st of the foll square.

DIRECTIONS
VERTICAL INSERTS
Ch 36 + ch 3 to turn (serves as first dc).
ROW 1: 1 dc in the 4th ch from hook, 1 dc in each ch across = 37 dc. Continue by foll chart, beg each row with ch 3, working the last dc of each row in the ch 3 of the previous row. Work first 7 rows for the lower edge of the zigzag, then work the 12 rows of repeat 12 times and end with the last 8 rows of the chart. Fasten off. Make 2.

EDGING
Ch 27 + ch 3 to turn (serves as first dc).
ROW 1: 1 dc in the 4th ch from hook, 1 dc in each ch across = 28 dc. Continue by foll chart. Work first 7 rows for the lower edge of the zigzag, then work the 12 rows of repeat 9 times and end with the last 8 rows of the chart. Work increases and decreases at right edge as shown on chart. For even edges, beg with ch 3, work the last dc of row in the ch 3 of the previous row. Fasten off.

FINISHING
Pin pieces to indicated measurements. Dampen and let dry. Cut the cotton fabric 33" wide and 40½" long. Along the upper edges and side edges, make a doubled hem about ¼" wide. Sew on the 2 vertical inserts to the right side of fabric spaced about 7" from the side edges using a zigzag stitch, beg ½" from lower edge. Cut out the fabric under the vertical inserts, leaving enough fabric to cover the zigzag stitches and sew hems. Sew on the lower edging with zigzag stitch and fold hem to inside and sew in place, covering the zigzag stitching. Cut out a strip of fabric 4" wide and 28¼" long. With right sides tog, sew fabric along long edges with ¼" seam allowance and turn right side out. Cut the fabric strip into 6 equal lengths. Fold in half and sew to wrong side of upper edge of curtain with zigzag stitch, placing 2 hangers on each section of fabric. Insert wooden dowel and hang.

KEY TO CHART
☐ = Open square
● = Filled square

Edging

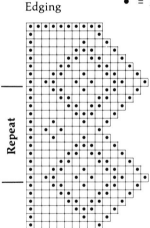

Vertical insert

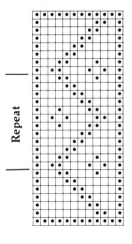

CURTAIN EDGING

See photo on page 45

SIZE

Edging: approx. 3¼" high and 18¾" long.
Insert: 2½" wide and 18¾" long.

MATERIALS

50 g crochet cotton thread. Steel crochet hook U.S. size 6. (U.K. size 2) White cotton fabric 20" x 40".

STITCHES USED

U.S. - Chain stitch (ch), slip stitch (sl st), single crochet (sc), double crochet (dc), triple crochet (tr). U.K. - chain stitch, slip stitch, double crochet, treble crochet, double treble crochet.

GAUGE

25 ch = 2½".

FILET CROCHET

Follow the chart.

DIRECTIONS

EDGING

Ch 25 + ch 4 to turn (which serves as the first open square).
ROW 1: 1 dc in the 7th ch from the hook, *ch 1, skip 1 ch, 1 dc in the foll dc*, work * to * twice, ch 3, skip 2 ch, 1 sc in the foll ch, ch 3, skip 2 ch, 1 dc in each of the foll 5 ch, ch 3, skip 2 ch, 1 sc in the foll ch, ch 3, skip 2 ch, 1 dc in the foll ch, ch 1, skip 1 ch, 1 dc in the last ch.
ROW 2: Ch 4 (= 1 dc + ch 1), 1 dc in the foll dc, ch 1, 1 dc in the foll ch 3 arc, ch 3, 1 sc in the foll dc, ch 5, skip 3 dc, 1 sc in the foll dc, ch 5, 1 sc in the foll dc, ch 3, 1 dc in the foll dc, ch 1, 1 dc in the foll dc, ch 1, 1 dc in the foll ch, ch 1, 1 tr in the same st and the last dc. Continue by foll chart until piece measures 18¾" or desired length. Fasten off. Along lower edge, work 1 row of picot as foll: join yarn at 1 point: 1 sc in the open square, *1 picot (= ch 3, 1 sc in the 3rd ch from hook), 1 sc in the foll open square*, rep * to * work to last point (1 sc, 1 picot, 1 sc in the open square). Fasten off.

INSERT

Ch 25 + ch 4 (= first open square).
ROWS 1 AND 2: Work the first and 2nd row same as above without inc at end of row 2. Continue by foll chart for insert until piece measures 18¾" or desired length. Fasten off.

FINISHING

Pin pieces to indicated measurements. Dampen and let dry. Cut fabric 18¾" wide and 3½" long with seam allowance. Cut a 2nd piece 18¾" wide and desired length with seam allowance. Make small hem around all edges of both pieces. Sew insert between pieces and sew on straight edge of edging to lower edge of small piece. Make a 2nd curtain.

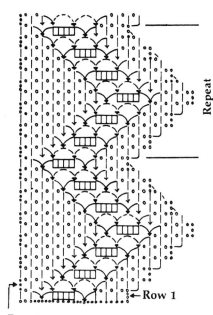

Row 2

Row 1

KEY TO CHART

o	= Ch
＼	= Slip stitch
▼	= Sc
I	= Dc
↓	= Dc in arc
⌐	= Tr
＼	= Ch 3 arc
⌒	= Ch 5 arc
⊞	= 5 dc in the arc

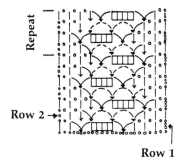

Repeat

Row 2

Row 1

TABLECLOTH EDGING

See photo on page 46

SIZE

Approx. 1".

MATERIALS

50 g crochet cotton thread. Steel crochet hook U.S. size 8. (U.K. size 3) Fabric for tablecloth of desired size.

STITCHES USED

U.S. - Chain stitch (ch), single crochet (sc), half double crochet (hdc), double crochet (dc). U.K. - chain stitch, double crochet, half treble, treble crochet.

GAUGE

12 squares in height and 14 squares in width = 4" x 4".

DIRECTIONS

Ch 12 + ch 5 to turn (serves as first dc).
ROW 1: 1 dc in the 6th ch from the hook, 1 dc in each of the foll 3 ch, ch 2, skip 2, 1 dc in the foll ch, ch 2, skip 2 ch, 1 dc in the foll ch, ch 1, skip 1 ch, 1 dc in the last ch.
ROW 2: Ch 4, 1 dc in the foll dc, ch 2, 1 dc in the foll dc, 2 dc in ch 2 arc, 1 dc in the foll dc, ch 2, skip 2 dc, 1 dc in the foll dc.
ROW 3: Ch 5, 1 dc in the foll dc, 2 dc in the ch 2 arc, 1 dc in the foll dc, ch 2, skip 2 dc, 1 dc in the foll dc, ch 2, 1 dc in the foll dc, ch 1, 1 dc in the 3rd ch of turning ch. Always rep rows 2 to 3 until desired length to corner.
CORNER ROW 1: Beg with the 2nd row of pat: ch 2, 1 sc in the foll dc, ch 2, 1 hdc in the foll dc, 2 dc in the ch 2 arc, 1 dc in the foll dc, ch 2, skip 2 dc, 1 dc in the foll dc.
CORNER ROW 2: Ch 5, 1 dc in the first dc, 2 dc in the ch 2 arc, 1 dc in the foll dc, ch 2, skip 2 dc, 1 hdc in the foll dc, ch 2, 1 sc in the foll sc, ch 1, 1 sc in the first ch of the turning ch.
CORNER ROW 3: Ch 2, 1 sc in the sc, ch 2, 1 hdc in the hdc, 2 dc in the ch 2 arc, 1 dc in the foll dc, ch 2, skip 2 dc, 1 dc in the foll dc. Continue by foll first 2 rows of pattern to the following corner and so on around, ending with a corner. Fasten off. Sew the ends tog.

FINISHING

Pin piece to indicated measurement. Dampen and let dry. Make a double hem around the edges of fabric to fit border and sew on border.

INSTRUCTIONS FOR PANELS AND DOILIES

3 WINDOW PANELS

See photo on page 4

SIZE

Approx. 11¾" x 16½".

MATERIALS

150 g crochet cotton thread. Steel crochet hook U.S. size 10. (U.K. size 4)

STITCHES USED

U.S. - Chain stitch (ch), double crochet (dc). U.K. - Chain stitch, treble crochet.

GAUGE

21 squares in height and width = 4" x 4".

FILET CROCHET

Follow the chart. An open square = 1 dc, ch 2, skip 2 sts, 1 dc. A filled square = 4 dc. On the chart, the last st of 1 square serves as the first st of the foll square.

DIRECTIONS

Ch 267 + ch 3 to turn (serves as first dc).
ROW 1: 1 dc in the 4th, 5th, and 6th ch from the hook (= 1 filled square), continue by foll chart = 89 squares. Beg each row with ch 3 and always work the last dc in the 3rd ch of the turning ch of the previous row. Continue by foll chart. Fasten off. Make 3 panels.

FINISHING

Pin pieces to indicated measurement. Dampen and let dry.

WINDOW HANGING

See photo on page 1

SIZE

Hanging size approx. 8½" x 8½". Frame size approx. 12½" x 13¾".

MATERIALS

20 g crochet cotton thread. Steel crochet hook U.S. size 12. (U.K. size 5)

STITCHES USED

U.S. - Chain stitch (ch), triple crochet (tr). U.K. - Chain stitch, double treble crochet.

GAUGE

15 squares in height and width = 4" x 4".

FILET CROCHET

Follow the chart. An open square = 1 tr, ch 3, skip 3 sts of previous row, 1 tr. A partially filled square = 1 tr, ch 1, skip 1 st of previous row, 1 tr, skip 1 st of previous row, ch 1, 1 tr. A completely filled square = 4 tr. On the chart, the last st of 1 square serves as the first st of the foll square.

DIRECTIONS

Ch 132 + ch 4 to turn (serves as first tr).
ROW 1: 1 tr in the 5th ch from the hook, 1 tr in next 3 ch, then foll chart for 33 rows. Beg each row with ch 4. Always work the last tr of every row in the 4th ch of the turning ch of the previous row. Fasten off.

FINISHING

Pin piece to indicated measurement. Dampen and let dry.

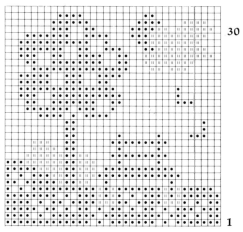

30

1

KEY TO CHARTS

☐ = Open square
• = Filled square
ıı = Partially filled square

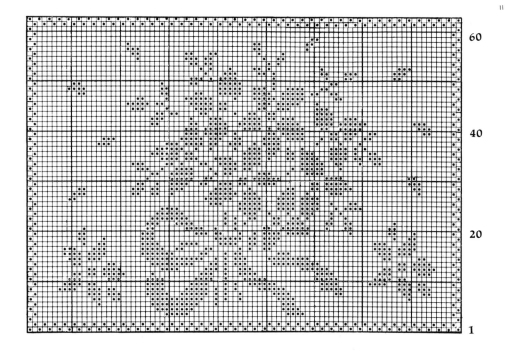

60

40

20

1

KEY TO CHART

☐ = Open square
• = Filled square

CURTAINS AND VALANCES

Filet crochet makes an ideal material for curtains and valances for several reasons. Filet crochet curtains shade much of the sun's glare without blocking light. The white cotton crochet thread is washable and will not fade. And, best of all, anyone who passes by

CURTAINS
AND
VALANCES

the outside of your home enjoys their beauty as much as you do on the inside.

*On the **previous page**, a diamond motif on a filet crochet valance makes a lovely frame for this country window. (see page 78 for directions)*

***Right**, a traditional Scandinavian snowflake motif is surrounded by small flakes of falling snow. (see page 78 for directions) A valance of this size is a good project for a rainy weekend, and can be adapted to any shape or size of window.*

CURTAINS AND VALANCES

Valances have been popular in Europe for centuries. Their popularity surely stems from the fact that they are quick and inexpensive to make and that they easily fit any window using a simple curtain rod. *A valance can be hung straight, such as the flower curtain **below**, or hung with gathers on the top, such as the cat valance at **bottom right**.*

This page features a festive group of valances and an edging made with colored crochet thread. ***Below left**, a yellow valance with flower motifs welcomes a sunny day. (see page 79 for directions)*

***Below right**, saucers, cream and sugars, and* a teapot make a charming border for a curtain edging. (see page 79 for directions)

***Opposite page, top**, a filet crochet designer converts her son's passion for gnomes into a decorative valance*

for his room. (see page 80 for directions)
Below right, a row of smiling cats prances across a filet crochet valance. (see page 81 for directions)

CURTAINS AND VALANCES

*T*he traditional, elegant beauty of designs from centuries ago is reflected in this filet crochet curtain with facing swans. (see page 81 for directions) The curtain looks like lace when the sun shines through and lets a flood of light into the room.

The swans could easily be bordered on the sides with open filet squares for a wider curtain. Or, if you have double windows, the motif could be divided in half and the swans would still face each other. This pattern would also be lovely on matching pillows.

CURTAINS AND VALANCES

L*eft, this set of curtains with blooming crocus motifs enhances the exuberance of spring days. (see page 81 for directions) To make a large, single curtain (like the swan curtain on the preceding page), the crocus pattern could be joined back into a single bouquet.*

Right, moving the curtain rod halfway down the window forms a creative variation of the traditional valance. The geometric motif in this filet crochet has a very contemporary look and serves as an inspirational reminder of your handiwork. (see page 82 for directions)

CURTAINS AND VALANCES

*L*eft, *in the tradition of Mediterranean living, a long curtain of filet crochet invites a summer breeze indoors while still providing privacy. The center bouquet of roses is bordered by smaller, curving flowers and several rows of open-work. (see page 83 for directions) This same curtain could fit a much wider doorway by simply spreading out some of the gathers.*

Right, *doves of peace fly through the welcoming archway of this very intricate example of filet crochet. (see page 87 for directions) Single design motifs from the curtain, such as one of the doves or the flower box, could be used to make match-ing accessories.*

CURTAINS AND VALANCES

*I*f you're looking for a smaller, less ambitious filet crochet curtain project to make, consider making a curtain just large enough to fit the window opening. Choose a filet motif that complements the pattern and texture of your full-length curtains, such as the snowflake pattern **shown left**. *(see page 87 for directions)*

Right, the perfect adornment for a garden window, this simple floral motif encourages sunlight to filter indoors. The curtain can also double as a tablecloth by simply removing the brass curtain hooks. *(see page 87 for directions)*

DIAMOND MOTIF VALANCE

See photo on page 65

SIZE

13¾" high, measured from a point to the top and 46¾" long.

MATERIALS

200 g fingering weight cotton thread. Steel crochet hook U.S. size 3. (U.K. size 1/0)

STITCHES USED

U.S. - Chain stitch (ch), slip stitch (sl st), double crochet (dc), triple crochet (tr). U.K. - Chain stitch, slip stitch, treble crochet, double treble crochet.

GAUGE

9 squares x 11 rows = 4" x 4".

FILET CROCHET

Follow the chart. An open square = 1 dc, ch 2, 1 dc. A filled square = 4 dc. On the chart, the last st of 1 square serves as the first st of the foll square.

DIRECTIONS

Ch 76 + ch 5 to turn (serves as first open square).

ROW 1: 1 dc in the 9th ch from the hook, *ch 2, skip 2 ch, 1 dc in the foll ch*, work * to * 6 times, 1 dc in each of the foll 15 ch, rep * to * 7 times, 1 dc in each of the foll 15 ch, ch 2, skip 2, 1 dc in the last ch of the hook, ch 2, 1 tr in the last dc of the chain. Turn.

ROW 2: Ch 6 (= 1 slanted increased square, 1 dc in the tr st of the previous row, ch 2, 1 dc in the foll dc, 2 dc in the open square, 1 dc in the foll dc, ch 2, skip 2 dc, 1 dc in the foll 10 dc, ch 2, skip 2 dc, 1 dc in the foll dc, 2 dc in the open square, 1 dc in the foll dc, *ch 2, skip 2, 1 dc*, work * to * 7 times, 1 dc in each of the foll 9 dc, ch 2, skip 2 dc, 1 dc in the foll dc, 2 dc in the open square, 1 dc in the foll dc, *ch 2, 1 dc in the foll dc*, work * to * 6 times. Turn.

Continue by foll chart 1. Increase and decrease for the points by foll detailed chart for increases and decreases. Use this chart when working section of chart 1 outlined in bold. Work until piece measures 46¾" long with 11 points or desired length. Do not fasten off.

Along the top edge, make the hangers. Work 2 sc in each of the squares along the top edge and in every 6th square

make a hanger: ch 20, 1 sc in the 4th ch from the hook, 1 sc in each of the foll 16 sc. Work 2 sc in the squares between hangers.

Along the lower edge, work as foll: in every slanted square: 1 sc, 1 picot (= ch 3, 1 sc in the 3rd ch from the hook), 1 sc. In every corner square between the points, work 1 sc. In every corner square of the point, work 1 sc, 1 picot, 1 sc, 1 picot.

FINISHING

Pin piece to indicated measurement. Dampen and let dry.

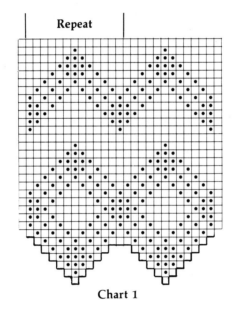

Repeat

Chart 1

KEY TO CHART

☐ = Open square
● = Filled square

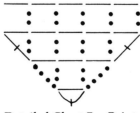

Detailed Chart For Points

KEY TO CHART

● = Ch

| = Dc

✝ = Tr

SNOWFLAKE VALANCE

See photo on page 66

SIZE

Approx. 9¾" x 45¼". Each point is 6½" wide.

MATERIALS

100 g crochet cotton thread. Steel crochet hook U.S. size 8. (U.K. size 3)

STITCHES USED

U.S. - Chain stitch (ch), double crochet (dc). U.K. - Chain stitch, treble crochet.

GAUGE

15 squares in height and width = 4" x 4".

FILET CROCHET

Follow the chart. An open square = 1 dc, ch 2, skip 2 sts of previous row, 1 dc. A filled square = 4 dc. On the chart, the last st of 1 square serves as the first st of the foll square.

DIRECTIONS

Ch 79 + ch 3 to turn (serves as first dc).

ROW 1: 1 dc in the 5th ch from the hook, 1 dc in each of the foll 74 ch, ch 2, skip 2, 1 dc in last ch = 1 open square.

ROW 2: Increase an open square at beg of row as foll: ch 8, 1 dc in the last dc of the previous row. 1 dc in each of the foll 3 sts (2 ch + 1 sc) = 1 filled square. *Skip 2 dc, 1 dc in the foll ch, ch 2*, work * to * 24 times. 1 dc in each of the last 3 sts = 1 filled square.

ROW 3: Ch 3, 1 filled square, 17 open squares, 1 filled square, 7 open squares, 1 filled square, 1 inc open square: ch 2, yo 4 times around hook, insert hook under the last worked dc, draw through 1 loop, draw through 2 loops 4 times. Continue by foll chart, rep rows 2 to 25 until piece measures 45¼" from beg = 7 points. End last repeat with the 24th row, then work row 1 once. Fasten off. If desired, make hangers evenly spaced along top edge. For each hanger: insert hook in top row, chain to twice desired length. Fold in half and fasten to first ch st.

Both American and British stitches are listed under STITCHES USED in each pattern, however, only the American terms are used in the text. British readers should convert these instructions to British terms as they work the projects.

FINISHING

Pin piece to indicated measurement. Dampen and let dry.

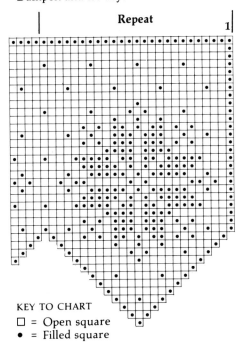

Repeat

KEY TO CHART

☐ = Open square
● = Filled square

YELLOW VALANCE

See photo on page 68, left

SIZE

Approx. 9¾" high x 30¼" long.

MATERIALS

90 g yellow crochet cotton thread. Steel crochet hook U.S. size 4. (U.K. size 1)

STITCHES USED

U.S. - Chain stitch (ch), slip stitch (sl st), single crochet (sc), double crochet (dc). U.K. - Chain stitch, slip stitch, double crochet, treble crochet.

GAUGE

30 sts (ch and dc) x 11 rows = 4" x 4".

FILET CROCHET

Follow the chart, which is worked sideways. There are 2 sizes in open and filled squares. A large open square = 1 dc, ch 2, skip 2 sts of previous row, 1 dc. A small open square = 1 dc, ch 1, skip 1 st of previous row, 1 dc. A large filled square = 4 dc. A small filled square = 3 dc. On the chart, the last st of 1 square serves as the first st of the foll square.

DIRECTIONS

Valance is worked sideways. Ch 65 + ch 3 (which serves as the first dc).
ROW 1: 1 dc in the 5th ch from the hook, 1 dc in each of the foll ch, ch 2, skip 2 ch, 1 dc in the foll ch, ch 1, skip 1, 1 dc in the foll ch, *ch 2, skip 2 ch, 1 dc in the foll ch*, work * to * 9 times, ch 1, skip 1 ch, 1 dc in the foll ch, ch 2, skip 2 ch, 1 dc in each of the foll 9 ch, ch 2, skip 2 ch, 1 dc in the foll ch, ch 1, skip 1 ch, 1 dc in the foll ch, work * to * 4 times, ch 9. Turn and continue by foll chart, beg with 1 dc in the 7th ch from the hook, ch 2, 1 dc in the foll dc and so on until piece measures 20¼" long (= 14 arcs). Fasten off. Along the arc edge, work 2

KEY TO CHART

· = Ch

| = Dc

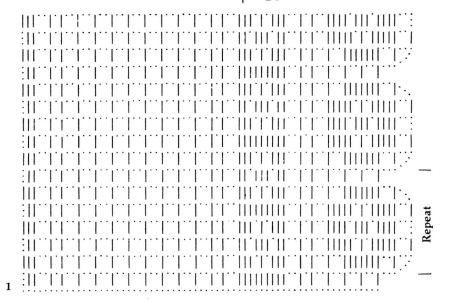

Repeat

sc in each open square and 3 sc in each slanted square. Fasten off. Along the upper edge, make hangers as foll: 1 sc in the corner square, *ch 20, 1 sc in the same square, 2 sc in each of the foll 2 squares, 1 sc in the foll square*, rep * to * across, end with ch 20, 1 hanger and sl st in the last square. Fasten off.

FINISHING

Pin piece to indicated measurement. Dampen and let dry.

TEAPOT VALANCE

See photo on page 68, right

SIZE

11½" wide and 59" long.

MATERIALS

175 g of fingering weight cotton thread. Steel crochet hook U.S. size 4. (U.K. size 1) Optional: Sheer fabric 12" wide and 60" long.

STITCHES USED

U.S. - Chain stitch (ch), double crochet (dc). U.K. - Chain stitch, treble crochet.

GAUGE

11 squares x 13 rows = 4" x 4".

FILET CROCHET

Follow the chart. An open square = 1 dc, ch 2, skip 2 sts of previous row, 1 dc. A filled square = 4 dc. On the chart, the last st of 1 square serves as the first st of the foll square. To increase 1 filled square + 1 open square at beg of a row: Ch 11, 1 dc in the 9th ch from the hook, 1 dc in each of the foll 2 ch, 1 dc in the last dc.

DIRECTIONS

Ch 97 + ch 5 to turn (serves as the first open square).
ROW 1: 1 dc in the 9th ch from the hook, ch 2, skip 2, 1 dc in the foll dc = 2 open squares, *1 dc in the foll 3 ch, ch 2, skip 2 ch, 1 dc in the foll ch*, rep * to * across 11 times total, ch 2, skip 2, 1 dc in the foll 4 ch, **ch 2, skip 2 ch, 1 dc in the foll ch**, work ** to ** 3 times, end with 1 dc in the last 3 ch = 32 squares. Turn.
ROW 2: Ch 5 = 1 open square, 1 dc in the last dc of the filled square, 2 dc in ch 2, 1 dc in the foll dc, *ch 2, skip 2, 1 dc in the foll dc*, work * to * 6 times total, **2 dc in ch 2, 1 dc in the foll dc, ch 2, skip 2, 1 dc in the foll dc**, work ** to ** across, end with ch 2, 1 dc in the 3rd ch of the turning ch. Continue by foll chart, beg with Row 3. Fasten off after last row.

FINISHING

Pin piece to indicated measurement. Dampen and let dry. Optional: Cut sheer fabric to match shape of finished crochet piece, allowing small seam allowance. Make a small hem along lower and side edges and make a pocket along top edge. Sew lining to crocheted piece.

KEY TO CHART

□ = Open square
● = Filled square

GNOME CURTAINS

See photo on page 69, top

SIZE

Approx. 13¾" x 35¾".

MATERIALS

140 g crochet cotton thread. Steel crochet hook U.S. size 4. (U.K. size 1)

STITCHES USED

U.S. - Chain stitch (ch), single crochet (sc), double crochet (dc). U.K. - Chain stitch, double crochet, treble crochet.

GAUGE

13 squares in height and 17 squares in width = 4" x 4".

FILET CROCHET

Follow the chart. An open square = 1 dc, ch 2, skip 2 sts of previous row, 1 dc. A filled square = 4 dc. On the chart, the last st of 1 square serves as the first st of the foll square.

DIRECTIONS

Ch 136 + ch 3 to turn (serves as first dc).

ROW 1: 1 dc in the 5th ch from the hook, 1 dc in each of the foll 2 ch = 1 filled square, *ch 2, skip 2 ch of the previous row, 1 dc = 1 open square, 1 dc in the foll 3 ch = 1 filled square*, work * to * 20 times, end with 2 open squares = 45 open and filled squares.

ROW 2: Ch 3, *ch 2, skip 2, 1 dc in the foll st*, work * to * 3 times, **2 dc in the ch 2 arc, 1 dc in the foll st (= 1 filled square above an open square), ch 2, skip 2, 1 dc in the foll dc (= 1 open square above a filled square)**, rep ** to **, end with 1 filled square inc: *wrap yarn around hook twice and insert in the last dc of previous row, yo, draw through 2 loops, yo, draw through 2 loops, yo, draw through 2 loops.* Rep * to * 2 more times. Continue by foll chart from rows 2 to 45, then rep rows 29 to 45, 7 times = 8 gnome motifs and 147 rows = 33¾", end with last 9 rows on chart. Work inc and dec as shown on chart. Fasten off.

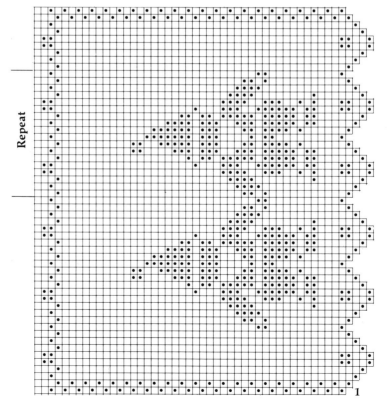

Repeat

1

KEY TO CHART

□ = Open square
● = Filled square

80

FINISHING

Pin piece to indicated measurement. Dampen and let dry. On top edge, work 1 row of sc by working 1 sc in each square. Make hangers every 6th square across top. For each hanger: in every 6th square, ch 25, 1 sc in the same square as first ch. Fasten off.

CAT MOTIF VALANCE

See photo on page 69, bottom

SIZE

11¾" high, measured from a point to the top and 37" long.

MATERIALS

150 g crochet cotton thread. Steel crochet hook U.S. size 6. (U.K. size 2) 9 rings.

STITCHES USED

U.S. - Chain stitch (ch), slip stitch (sl st), double crochet (dc). U.K. - Chain stitch, slip stitch, treble crochet.

GAUGE

17 squares x 14 rows = 4" x 4".

FILET CROCHET

Follow the chart. An empty square = 1 dc, ch 1, skip 1 st of previous row, 1 dc.

A filled square = 3 dc. On the chart, the last st of 1 square serves as the first st of the foll square.

DIRECTIONS

Ch 91 + ch 3 (serves as the first dc).
ROW 1: 1 dc in the 5th ch from the hook, 1 dc in the foll ch (= 1 filled square), *ch 1, skip 1, 1 dc in the foll ch*, rep * to * 41 times, 1 dc in the foll ch 2, ch 1, skip 1, 1 dc in the last ch. Continue by foll chart. Turn and beg every row with ch 3 which serves as the first dc of the first filled square. Work increases and decreases by foll chart. Work the first 10 rows, work repeat shown on chart 3 times, end by working first row once. Fasten off.

FINISHING

Pin piece to indicated measurement. Dampen and let dry. Attach 9 rings along top, evenly spaced.

KEY TO CHART

☐ = Open square
● = Filled square

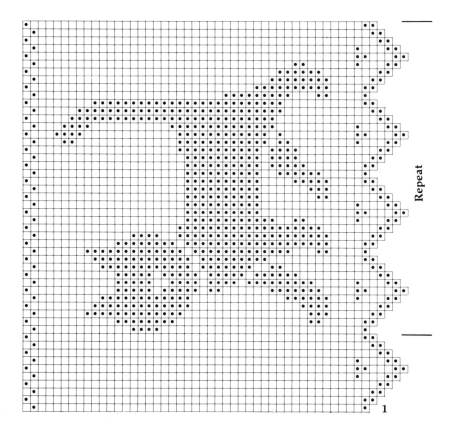

Repeat

1

SWAN CURTAINS

See photo on page 70

SIZE

Approx. 41½" x 35½".

MATERIALS

350 g crochet cotton thread. Steel crochet hook U.S. size 2. (U.K. size 2/0)

STITCHES USED

U.S. - Chain stitch (ch), double crochet (dc). U.K. - Chain stitch, treble crochet.

GAUGE

9 squares wide x 11 rows high = 4" x 4".

FILET CROCHET

Follow the chart. An open square = 1 dc, ch 2, skip 2 sts of previous row, 1 dc. A filled square = 4 dc. On the chart, the last st of 1 square serves as the first st of the foll square.

DIRECTIONS

Ch 250 + ch 3 to turn (serves as first dc).
ROW 1: 1 dc in the 5th ch from the hook, 2 dc, *1 dc, ch 2, skip 2 ch, 3 dc*, rep * to * across row = alternately 1 filled square, 1 open square, end with 1 filled square = 83 squares. Beg each row that beg with a filled square with ch 3 and each row that beg with an open square with ch 5. Always work the last dc in the 3rd ch of the turning ch of previous row. Continue by foll chart until piece measures 41½" from beg or to desired length. Fasten off.

FINISHING

Pin piece to indicated measurement. Dampen and let dry.

See chart on page 82

TULIP CURTAIN

See photo on page 72

SIZE

15¾" x 23½".

MATERIALS

200 g crochet cotton thread. Steel crochet hook U.S. size 8. (U.K. size 3)

STITCHES USED

U.S. - Chain stitch (ch), double crochet (dc). U.K. - Chain stitch, treble crochet.

GAUGE

15 squares in height and width = 4" x 4".

BOW-TIE CURTAINS

See photo on page 73

SIZE
Approx. width and height of pat rep 4½". Curtain approx. 19¾" x 51¼".

MATERIALS
350 g crochet cotton thread. Steel crochet hook U.S. size 4. (U.K. size 1)

STITCHES USED
U.S. - Chain stitch (ch), double crochet (dc). U.K. - Chain stitch, treble crochet.

GAUGE
12 squares x 12 rows = 4" x 4".

FILET CROCHET
Follow the chart. An open square = 1 dc, ch 2, skip 2 sts of previous row, 1 dc. A filled square = 4 dc. On the chart, the last st of 1 square serves as the first st of the foll square.

DIRECTIONS
Ch 183 + ch 3 to turn (serves as first dc).
ROW 1: 1 dc in the 4th ch from the hook, 1 dc in each of the foll ch = 184 dc.

Continue by foll chart working from beg of row to right arrow, then rep between arrows 3 times, then work to end of row. Rep rows 1 to 15 once, rep rows 2 to 15, 9 times, then end with rows 16 to 29. Beg each even row with ch 3 and always work the last dc in the

3rd ch of the turning ch of previous row. Work inc and dec as shown on chart. Fasten off.

FINISHING
Pin piece to indicated measurement. Dampen and let dry.

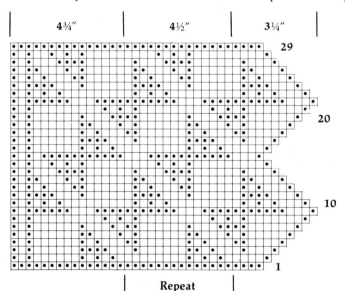

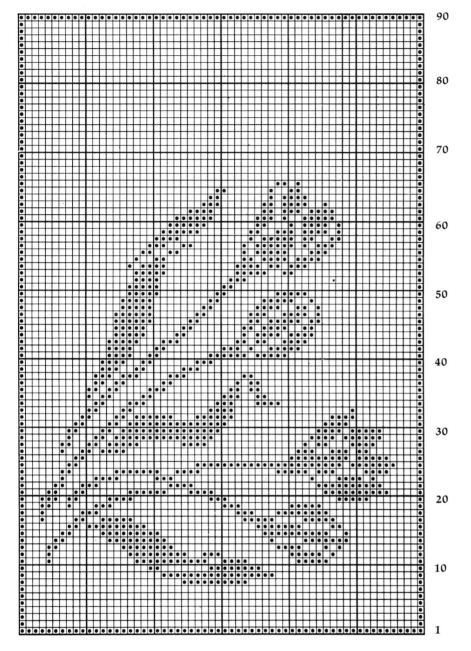

KEY TO CHART

□ = Open square
● = Filled square

Tulip Curtain, *Continued*

FILET CROCHET

Follow the chart. An open square = 1 dc, ch 2, skip 2 sts of previous row, 1 dc. A filled square = 4 dc. On the chart, the last st of 1 square serves as the first st of the foll square.

DIRECTIONS

Ch 180 + ch 3 to turn (serves as first dc).

ROW 1: 1 dc in 4th ch from hook, 1 dc in each ch across = 181 dc. Continue by foll chart, beg each row with ch 3, working the last dc of each row in the ch 3 of the previous row. Work rows 2 to 90 of chart, then fasten off. Make the 2nd piece by rev chart (beg first row at left edge of chart).

FINISHING

Pin pieces to indicated measurement. Dampen and let dry.

FLORAL CURTAIN

See photo on page 74

SIZE

Approx. 86½" x 106¼".

MATERIALS

1500 g crochet cotton thread. Steel crochet hook U.S. size 10. (U.K. size 4)

STITCHES USED

U.S. - Chain stitch (ch), slip stitch (sl st), single crochet (sc), triple crochet (tr).
U.K. - Chain stitch, slip stitch, double crochet, double treble crochet.

GAUGE

13 squares x 13 rows = 4" x 4".

FILET CROCHET

Follow the chart. An open square = 1 tr, ch 3, skip 3 sts of previous row, 1 tr. A filled square = 5 tr. An arc square = 1 tr, ch 3, 1 sc, ch 3, 1 tr. On the chart, the last st of 1 square serves as the first st of the foll square.

DIRECTIONS

Beg by working each of the 7 lower arcs and 2 corners separately for first 3 rows of chart. For each arc, ch 63. For each corner, ch 47. In the 11th ch from the hook work 1 tr = 1 open square. Continue by foll chart for each arc and corner. Ch 4 at the beg of each row. Work the last tr of every row in the 4th ch of the turning ch of the previous row. Work increases and decreases as shown on chart. Inc at beg of row: for each inc square, ch 4. For the last inc square: ch 10. Work the first tr in the 11th ch from the hook. Inc at the end of the row: For each new square, ch 3, wrap yarn around the hook twice, insert hook in the last tr of the previous row, *yo and draw through 2 loops*, rep * to * until 1 loop remains. For additional inc squares insert hook in the previous inc tr. Decreases: At beg of row, sl st over desired number of dec squares. At end of row, leave desired number of dec squares unworked.

After the 5th row of chart, ch 3 between each arc and sl st to foll arc. When 6th row of chart is complete = 286 filet squares. Continue by foll chart. After row 175, you are at center of chart. Now work from rows 174 to row 1, working each arc and corner separately on last 5 rows. Fasten off.

FINISHING

Pin piece to indicated measurement, pinning frequently along each edge. Dampen and let dry.

See chart on pages 84 - 85

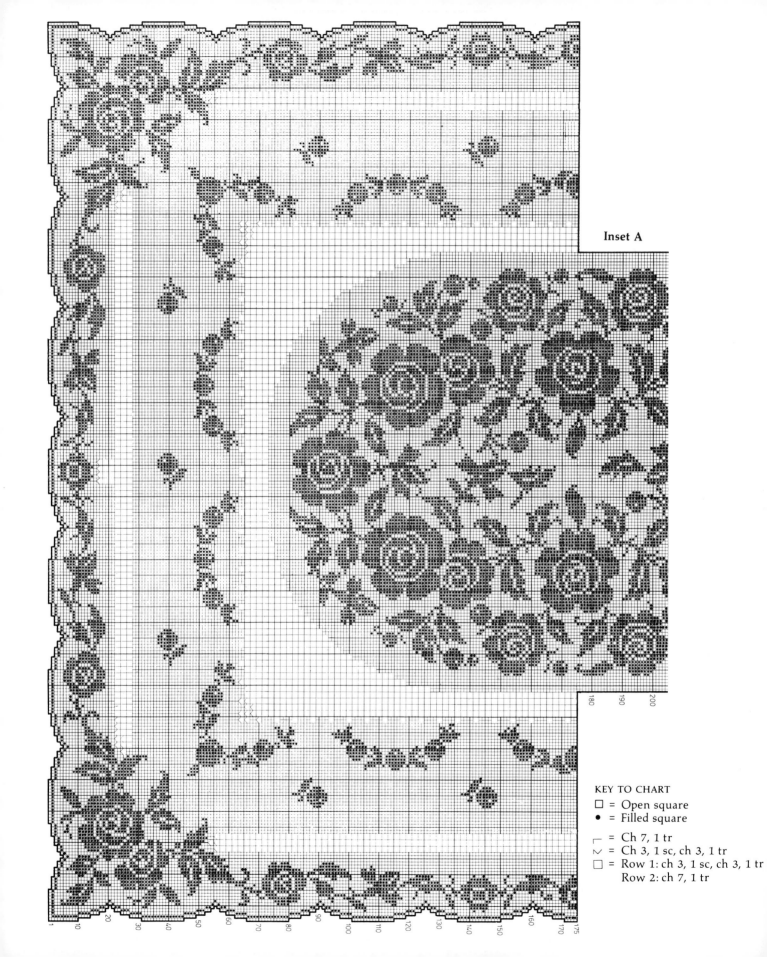

Inset A

KEY TO CHART

☐ = Open square
● = Filled square

└ = Ch 7, 1 tr
⋎ = Ch 3, 1 sc, ch 3, 1 tr
☐ = Row 1: ch 3, 1 sc, ch 3, 1 tr
Row 2: ch 7, 1 tr

Inset A

277
270
260
250
240
230
220
210
200
190
180

161

150

140

130

120

110

100

90

80

70

60

50

40

30

20

10

1

DOVE CURTAIN

See photo on page 75

SIZE

Approx. 45¼" x 60¼".

MATERIALS

600 g crochet cotton thread. Steel crochet hook U.S. size 2. (U.K. size 2/0)

STITCHES USED

U.S. - Chain stitch (ch), double crochet (dc). U.K. - Chain stitch, treble crochet.

GAUGE

10½ squares in height and width = 4" x 4".

FILET CROCHET

Follow the chart. An open square = 1 dc, ch 2, skip 2 sts of previous row, 1 dc. A filled square = 4 dc. On the chart, the last st of 1 square serves as the first st of the foll square.

DIRECTIONS

Ch 363 + ch 3 to turn (serves as first dc). Mark every 50th ch st with a strand of a different color yarn to use as a guide in counting.
ROW 1: 1 dc in the 4th ch from the hook, 1 dc in each of the ch sts = 364 dc. Continue by foll chart from rows 2 to 161. Beg each row with ch 3 and always work the last dc in the 3rd ch of the turning ch of previous row. Fasten off.

FINISHING

Pin piece to indicated measurement. Dampen and let dry.

KEY TO CHART

☐ = Open square
● = Filled square

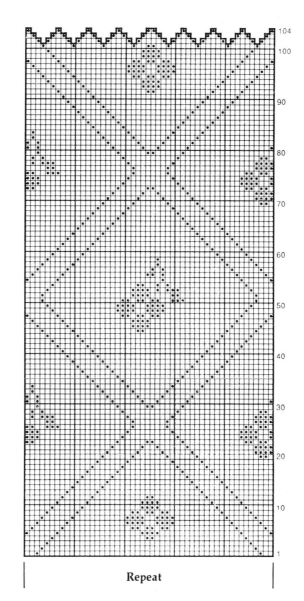

Repeat

KEY TO CHART

☐ = Open square
● = Filled square

FLOWER CURTAIN

See photo on page 77

SIZE

Approx. 27½" wide x 43¼" long.

MATERIALS

350 g crochet cotton thread. Steel crochet hook U.S. size 6 (U.K. size 2).

STITCHES USED

U.S. - Chain stitch (ch), double crochet (dc). U.K. - Chain stitch, treble crochet.

GAUGE

21 squares in height and width = 4" x 4".

FILET CROCHET

Follow the chart. An open square = 1 dc, ch 2, skip 2 sts of previous row. A filled square = 4 dc. On the chart, the last st of 1 square serves as the first st of the foll square.

DIRECTIONS

Ch 450 + ch 3 to turn (serves as first dc).
ROW 1: 1 dc in the 8th ch from the hook (= 1 open square), continue by working chart between arrows 3 times = 150 squares. Beg each row with ch 3 and always work the last dc in the 3rd ch of the turning ch of the previous row. Work the last 3 rows by working each point separately. Fasten off.

FINISHING

Pin piece to indicated measurement. Dampen and let dry.

SNOWFLAKE CURTAIN

See photo on page 76

SIZE

Approx. 33½" wide x 43¼" long.

MATERIALS

300 g crochet cotton thread. Steel crochet hook U.S. size 7 (U.K. size 2½).

STITCHES USED

U.S. - Chain stitch (ch), double crochet (dc). U.K. - Chain stitch, treble crochet.

GAUGE

15 squares x 15 rows = 4" x 4".

FILET CROCHET

Follow the chart. An open square = 1 dc, ch 2, skip 2 sts of previous row. A

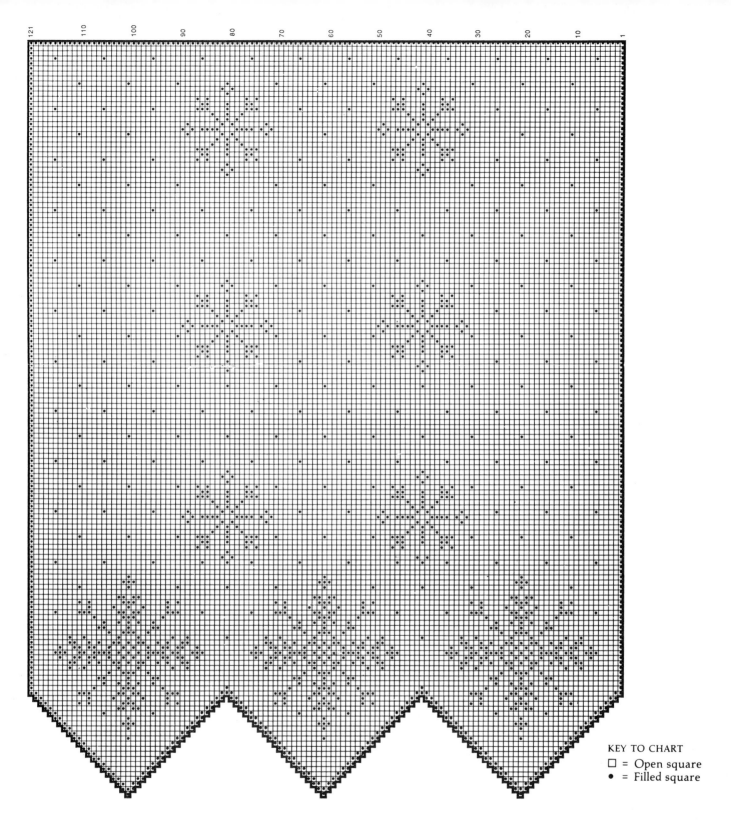

KEY TO CHART
□ = Open square
• = Filled square

filled square = 4 dc. On the chart, the last st of 1 square serves as the first st of the foll square.

DIRECTIONS
Ch 390 + ch 3 to turn (serves as first dc).

ROW 1: 1 dc in the 4th ch from the hook and work 1 dc, work 1 dc in each ch across = 390 dc + turning ch. Beg rows without incs or decs with ch 3. Work inc and dec by foll chart. When chart is complete, fasten off.

FINISHING
Pin piece to indicated measurement. Dampen and let dry.

BEDROOM AND NURSERY

A s the demands of 20th century living become more and more hectic, people have begun to value places in their homes where they can relax and retreat. Rooms such as the bedroom are being decorated with more attention, and designers from the clothing

BEDROOM AND NURSERY

industry have rushed
to produce *bedroom
ensembles high in style
and price.*

As shown on the
previous page, even
*a small inset of filet
crochet transforms an
ordinary white pillow-
case into something
special. The filet's
pattern matches the*

handwork on the
*sheeting, and the result
is a crisp, comfortable
style.* (see page 105 for
directions)

*This bedspread of filet
crochet (see page 105
for directions) showcases
the beauty of the
designer's handwork
and the natural beauty
of the wood furniture.*

BEDROOM AND NURSERY

*O*ne of the most enchanting aspects of filet crochet is its amazing design flexibility. Part of this flexibility comes from the tradition of using white crochet thread, which allows a finished product to be placed over fabrics of a solid color for a completely different look. If you like to change your bedroom colors with the seasons, it's as simple as draping your filet bedspread over a chair while you replace your old comforter or sheet with one of a new color.

*Here, a crocheter's love for pastel colors and fresh flowers is unquestionably a **tour de force** in skill and patience. (see page 106 for directions)*

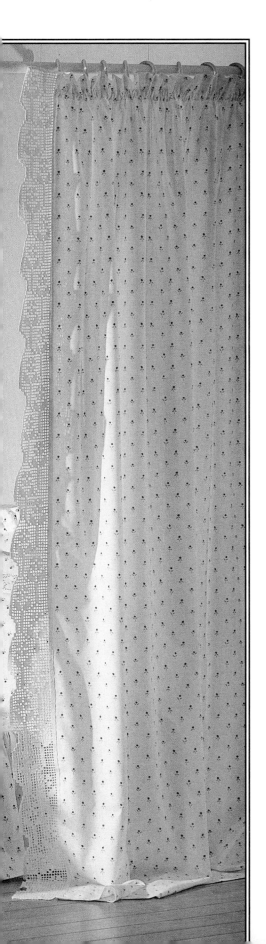

BEDROOM AND NURSERY

eft, a creative designer transformed ordinary bed sheets and pillows into a romantic bedroom nook with the help of several filet crochet insets and edgings. (see page 106 for directions)

***Below**, a close-up view of the filet patterns* reveals: *a gaggle of geese for the comforter edging; a row of flower buds for the pillowcase inset; a vertical repeat of stemmed flowers with leaves for the curtain edging. (see page 106 for directions)*

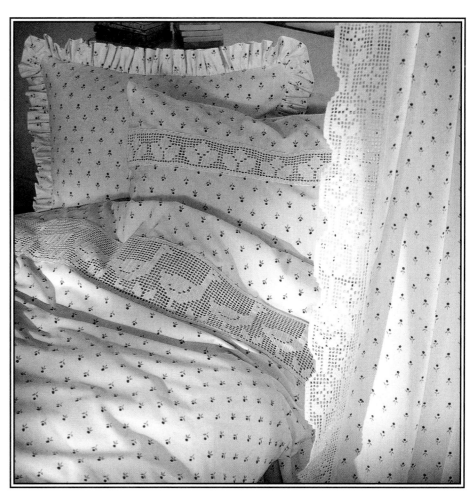

BEDROOM AND NURSERY

Filet crochet edgings make the perfect accent for a baby's first bed. A filet edging on the baby's comforter shown here uses a cloud motif to complement the cloud pattern in the canopy's fabric; while the canopy's filet edging uses a star motif to complement the star pattern in the fabric of the bassinette's skirt. (see pages 107 and 108 for directions)

The bassinette shown here is actually an old baby carriage that has been creatively covered with fabric. A search through used furniture stores in your own neighborhood may yield an old carriage or bassinette with conversion potential.

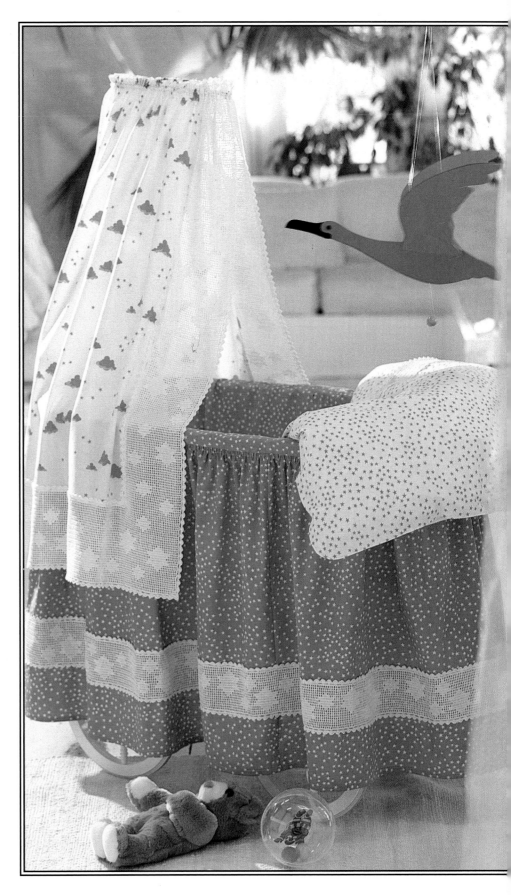

BEDROOM AND NURSERY

For the nursery shown here, the decor is based on a heart motif repeated in filet crochet projects. **Above left**, a valance decorated with hearts creates a lace-like effect when the sun shines through the window. **Below left**, blocks of filet crochet are made separately and then crocheted together to form a coverlet. As the baby grows, additional rows of heart blocks can be added to increase the size.

Any extra squares you make to test your gauge or for practice can be made into a pin cushion, **far right**, or crocheted together to make larger, decorative pillows, **right**. (see pages 109 and 110 for directions)

98

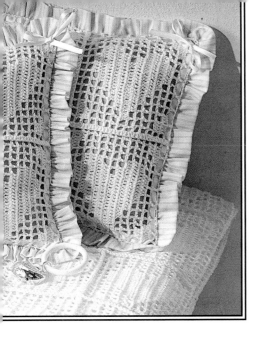
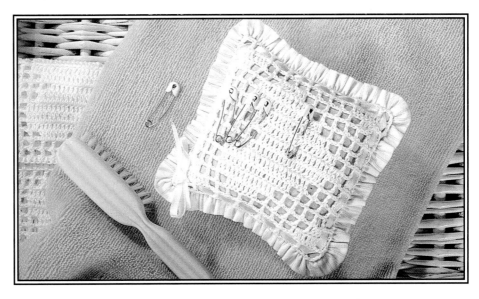
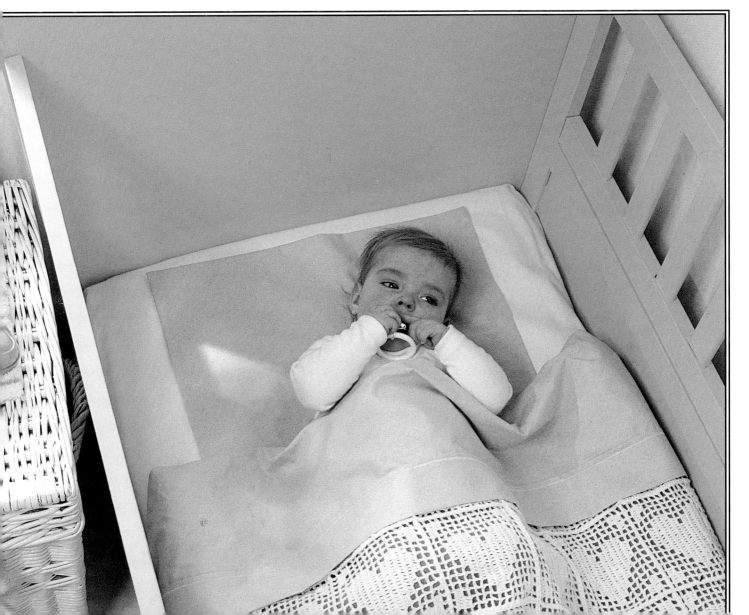

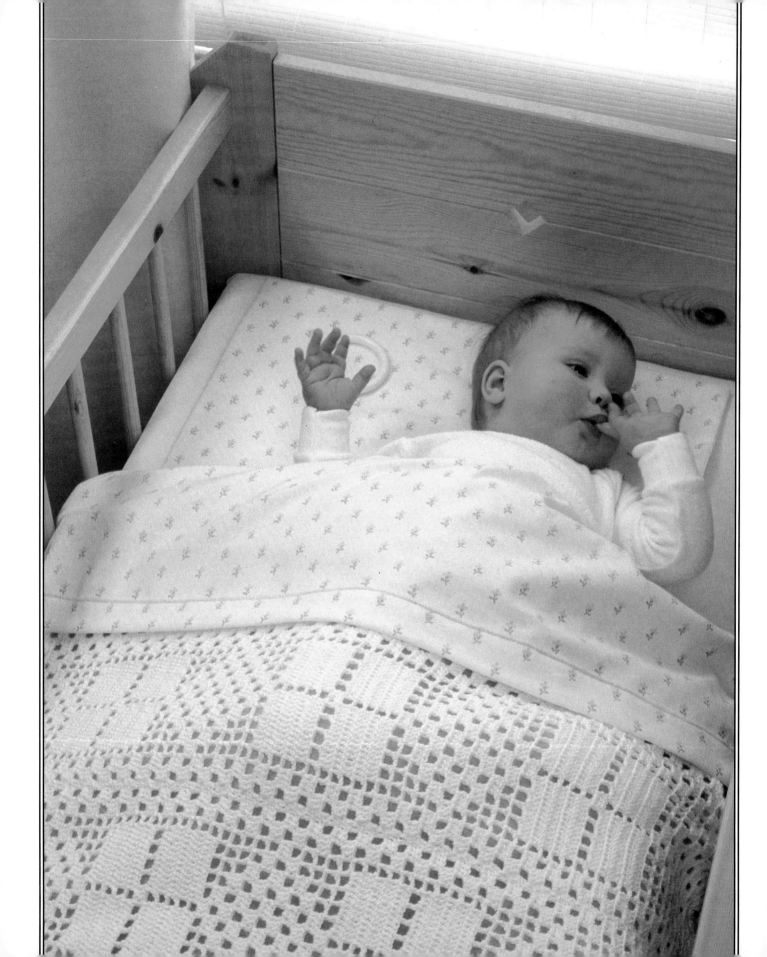

BEDROOM AND NURSERY

Another possible decor style for baby's bedroom is this Amish-inspired geometric motif. (see page 110 for directions) The design can be made as a thin band for adorning a sheet, shown **below**, or as a shelf or pillow edging. A wider band of the same design can be made with the same directions by using a thicker crochet thread or yarn and a larger hook.

Left, a coverlet using the same motif is made in strips and then attached with single crochet stitches. (see page 111 for directions) Additional rows can easily be added as the baby moves to a larger crib or bed.

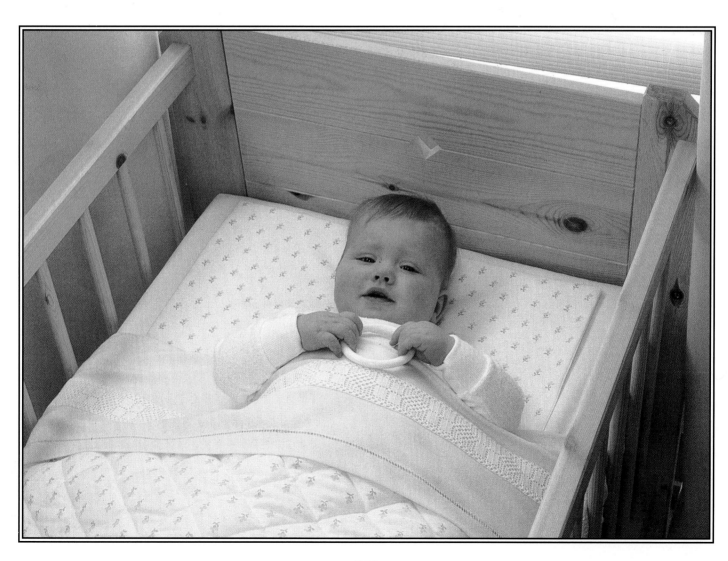

BEDROOM AND NURSERY

A winter snowflake pattern creates a bright, summer ambiance in this filet crocheter's bedroom, *below*. The tablecloth (see page 140 for directions) and pillowcases (see page 111 for directions) are made from single filet squares that are joined together after completion. Making the projects in this manner allows beginners to make relatively large projects (such as the tablecloth shown here) in small, easy-to-handle squares, and the work is small enough to carry with you on trips and visits.

Right, strips of filet crochet with a geometric motif add just the right touch of class to a teenager's room. The filet strips are used as insets on white pillowcases and a sheet, and then backed with pink fabric. (see page 111 for directions) Choose the backing color to match other colors of the room's decor, and simply change to a new backing color if the design scheme changes.

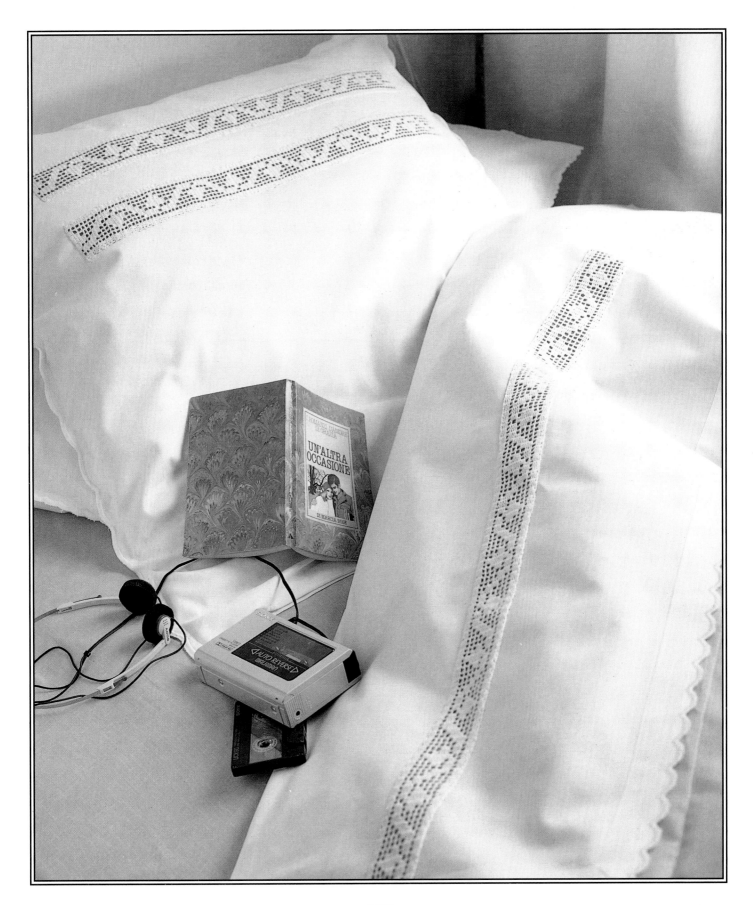

BEDROOM AND NURSERY

Pillow shams, long appreciated for the cozy atmosphere they add to a bedroom, are easy to embellish with filet crochet. Any of the decorating methods discussed in this chapter — edgings, insets, colored backings — can be incorporated into a pillow sham design.

Left, strips of filet with rose and wreath motifs are lined with a blue fabric and sewn onto the sham. (see page 112 for directions) Two rows of blue ribbon are used as an extra touch. Tip: If one of your first filet projects refuses to block evenly, sew a strip of ribbon over the edges, as shown on the wreath motif pillow, to hide uneven edges.

PILLOW BORDER

See photo on page 89

SIZE

Approx. 3½" wide.

MATERIALS

100 g crochet cotton thread. Steel crochet hook U.S. size 8. (U.K. size 3) Pillow case.

STITCHES USED

U.S. - Chain stitch (ch), single crochet (sc), double crochet (dc). U.K. - Chain stitch, double crochet, treble crochet.

GAUGE

12 squares x 12 rows = 4" x 4".

FILET CROCHET

Follow the chart. An open square = 1 dc, ch 2, skip 2 sts of previous row, 1 dc. A filled square = 4 dc. On the chart, the last st of 1 square serves as the first st of the foll square.

DIRECTIONS

Ch 58 + ch 3 (which serves as the first dc).
ROW 1: 1 sc in the 5th ch from the hook, and foll chart, beg at point A. Work by repeating chart from point A to B to desired length to beg of first corner, then work from point B to C. Beg each

row with ch 3 and work last dc in the 3rd ch of the turning ch of the previous row. Fasten off. Join yarn to edge of piece at point A2 and work from point A2 to B2, then A to B to desired length to beg of 2nd corner and continue around all 4 corners. Fasten off. Sew ends tog.

FINISHING

Pin piece to indicated measurement. Dampen and let dry. Sew filet piece to top of pillow case with very fine stitches.

BEDSPREAD

See photo on page 90

SIZE

Approx. 86½ x 80" (full size bed). Each panel is 8¼" wide, each motif is 7" long. The border is 3¼" wide.

MATERIALS

1600 g crochet cotton thread. Steel crochet hook U.S. size 4. (U.K. size 1) [For a twin size bed 86½" x 56": 1250 g crochet cotton thread. For a queen size bed 86½" x 96¼": 2000 g crochet cotton thread.]

STITCHES USED

U.S. - Chain stitch (ch), single crochet (sc), double crochet (dc). U.K. - Chain stitch, double crochet, treble crochet.

GAUGE

12 squares x 12 rows = 4" x 4".

FILET CROCHET

Follow the charts. An open square = 1 dc, ch 2, skip 2 sts of previous row, 1 dc. A filled square = 4 dc. On the chart, the last st of 1 square serves as the first st of the foll square.

DIRECTIONS

Worked in panels with a border on sides. For twin size, make 6 panels; for full size, make 9 panels; for queen size make 11 panels.

PANEL

Ch 76 + ch 5 (which serves as the first open square).
ROW 1: 1 dc in the 8th ch from the hook, *ch 2, skip 2 ch, 1 dc in the foll ch*, rep * to * across = 25 open squares. Turn. Continue by foll chart, beg each row with ch 3 and work last dc in the 3rd ch

of the turning ch of the previous row. Rep row 1 to 23. Work until piece measures 86½" from beg. Fasten off.

BORDER

Ch 28 + ch 5 (which serves as the first open square).
ROW 1: 1 dc in the 8th ch from the hook, *ch 2, skip 2 ch, 1 dc in the foll ch, 3 dc*, work * to * 4 times. At the beg of the foll row, inc 1 open square by beg row with ch 8, work first dc in the last dc of the previous row. At the end of the foll row, dec 1 square by leaving last square unworked. Continue by foll chart. Work until piece measures 86½" from beg. Fasten off. Make a 2nd border.

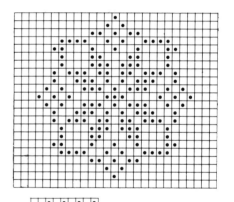

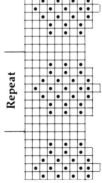

KEY TO CHART

☐ = Open square
● = Filled square

FINISHING

Pin pieces to indicated measurements. Dampen and let dry. Make chains about 120" long and sew the panels tog

Both American and British stitches are listed under STITCHES USED in each pattern, however, only the American terms are used in the text. British readers should convert these instructions to British terms as they work the projects.

B2 A2

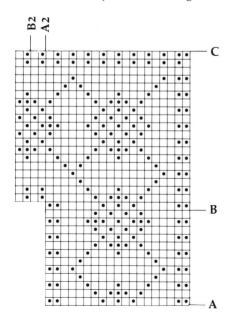

C

B

A

KEY TO CHARTS

☐ = Open square
● = Filled square

by sewing through 1 open square of 1 panel to corresponding square of 2nd panel and so on. Sew on borders in the same way. Secure ends of the sewing chains.

BEDSPREAD

See photo on page 92

See instructions for Floral Curtain on page 83

BED CURTAIN EDGING

See photo on page 94

SIZE

Bed curtain approx. 90¼" x 67½". Border 90¼" long and 4¾" wide.

MATERIALS

Approx. 250 g crochet cotton thread. Steel crochet hook U.S. size 4. (U.K. size 1) Laura Ashley fabric "Cottage Sprig" 48" wide and 8½ yards long. 4 yds of seam binding.

STITCHES USED

U.S. - Chain stitch (ch), double crochet (dc). U.K. - Chain stitch, treble crochet.

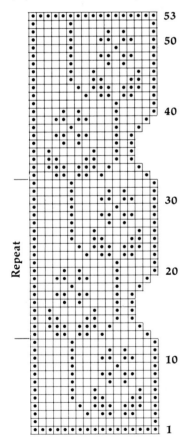

KEY TO CHART

□ = Open square   • = Filled square

GAUGE

14½ squares in height and width = 4" x 4".

FILET CROCHET

Follow the chart. An open square = 1 dc, ch 2, skip 2 sts of previous row, 1 dc. A filled square = 4 dc. On the chart, the last st of 1 square serves as the first st of the foll square.

DIRECTIONS

Ch 51 + ch 3 to turn (serves as first dc). ROW 1: 1 dc in the 4th ch from the hook, 1 dc in each ch across = 52 dc. Continue by foll chart from rows 2 to 32. Beg each row with ch 3 and always work the last dc in the 3rd ch of the turning ch of previous row. Work inc and dec as shown on chart. Rep rows 13 to 32, 14 times, then work rows 33 to 53. Fasten off.

FINISHING

Pin piece to indicated measurement. Dampen and let dry. For each side of the bed curtains, cut a piece 2¾ yds long and 47¼" wide and another ¾ yds long and 23½" wide. Make a ¾" seam with right sides tog along 1 long edge. Make a double hem ¼" wide along each long side. On lower edge make a hem about ¾" wide, then fold 4" to inside and slip stitch in place. Make a hem ¾" along the top edge, then turn 3¼" from top of hem, run a basting thread and gather so that curtain measures 72" wide. Sew on seam binding over the gathering to keep in place. Sew on the border with the border placed over the outer ⅛" of the curtain. Make a 2nd curtain.

BED LINEN EDGING

See photo on page 95

SIZE

Comforter cover approx. 55" x 78½". Border 6½" wide. Pillows about 23½" x 27½". Border 3¼" wide.

MATERIALS

Approx. 150 g crochet cotton thread. Steel crochet hook U.S. size 6. (U.K. size 2) Laura Ashley fabric "Cottage Sprig" comforter cover and pillow cases. Apple green lining fabric 8¼" x 56¾" and 4¾" x 29".

STITCHES USED

U.S. - Chain stitch (ch), double crochet (dc). U.K. - Chain stitch, treble crochet.

GAUGE

14 squares in height and width = 4" x 4".

FILET CROCHET

Follow the chart. An open square = 1 dc, ch 2, skip 2 sts of previous row, 1 dc. A filled square = 4 dc. On the chart, the last st of 1 square serves as the first st of the foll square.

DIRECTIONS

COMFORTER COVER BORDER

Ch 72 + ch 3 to turn (serves as first dc). ROW 1: 1 dc in the 4th ch from the hook, 1 dc in 5th and 6th ch, *ch 2, skip 2 ch, 1 dc*, rep * to * 21 times. In the last 3 ch, work 1 dc in each ch. Continue by foll chart from rows 2 to 39. Beg each row with ch 3 and always work the last dc in the 3rd ch of the turning ch of previous row. Rep rows 22 to 39, 7 times, then work rows 40 to 60. Fasten off.

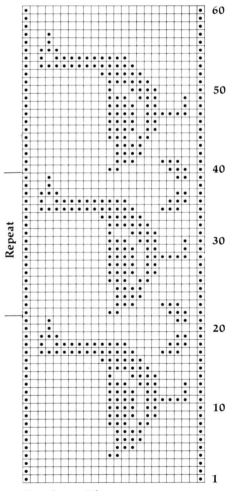

Comforter Edging

KEY TO CHART

□ = Open square   • = Filled square

PILLOW INSERT

Ch 36 + ch 3 to turn (serves as first dc).

ROW 1: 1 dc in the 4th ch from the hook, 1 dc in 5th and 6th ch, *ch 2, skip 2 ch, 1 dc*, rep * to * 9 times. In the last 3 ch, work 1 dc in each ch. Continue by foll chart from rows 2 to 25. Beg each row with ch 3 and always work the last dc in the 3rd ch of the turning ch of previous row. Rep rows 13 to 25, 5 times, then work rows 26 to 39. Fasten off.

FINISHING
Pin pieces to indicated measurement. Dampen and let dry.

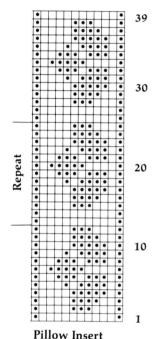

Pillow Insert

KEY TO CHART
□ = Open square
● = Filled square

COMFORTER COVER
Open side seams 6" from the top edge of comforter cover to 10¾" from top edge. Make a ¾" hem along the top and lower edge of the larger piece of green lining material and sew on crochet piece (crochet border will overlap lining). Sew on border to comforter cover, inserting ends in seams and closing seams.

PILLOW CASE
Beginning 2¾" from the top edge of pillow case to 7¼" from top edge, open the side seams. Make a ¾" hem along the top and lower edge of the smaller piece of green lining material and sew on crochet piece (crochet border will overlap lining). Sew on to pillow case, inserting ends in seams and close seams.

BASSINETTE LINENS
See photo on page 96

SIZE
Pillow approx. 13¾" x 13¾". Comforter 31½" x 31½". Border approx. 3¼" wide.

MATERIALS
40 g crochet cotton thread. Steel crochet hook U.S. size 8. (U.K. size 3) 3 yds white cotton with star motif 36" wide. Light blue lining fabric 4" x 16" and 4" x 33".

STITCHES USED
U.S. - Chain stitch (ch), slip stitch (sl st), single crochet (sc), double crochet (dc).
U.K. - Chain stitch, slip stitch, double crochet, treble crochet.

GAUGE
24 squares in height and width = 4" x 4".

FILET CROCHET
Follow the chart. An open square = 1 dc, ch 1, 1 dc. A filled square = 3 dc. On the chart, the last st of 1 square serves as the first st of the foll square.

DIRECTIONS
Ch 172.
ROW 1: 1 dc in the 6th ch from the hook, *ch 1, skip 1 of previous row, 1 dc*, rep * to * across = 84 squares.
ROWS 2 to 12: Work the pattern repeat between the double arrows once, then work between the single arrows once. Foll the chart. Beg each row with ch 3. Work the last dc in the 3rd ch at beg of previous row. Fasten off. Then work border around all edges by foll chart, sl st to join each round. Fasten off.

FINISHING
Pin piece to indicated measurement. Dampen and let dry. Cut a piece of star motif fabric 12½" x 15¼" and a 2nd piece 19¾" x 15¼". With right sides tog, sew the smaller piece of blue lining fabric to one 15¼" end of each piece of star fabric, making a ¾" seam. On the other 2 ends, make a ¼" double seam. With right sides tog, 4¼" from the top of the blue lining, iron a fold (to indicate

KEY TO CHART
□ = Open square   ● = Filled square

the top of the pillow.) 13¾" from the fold, iron a 2nd fold (to indicate the bottom of the pillow.) The fabric will overlap on the back by 4". Sew side seams, right sides tog, with a seam allowance of ¾". Turn pillow right side out. Make a ¼" hem around all edges. Sew on the crochet border over lining fabric by hand.

DIRECTIONS
COMFORTER COVER
Ch 376.
ROW 1: 1 dc in the 6th ch from the hook, *ch 1, skip 1 of previous row, 1 dc*, rep * to * across = 186 squares.
ROWS 2 to 12: Work the pattern repeat from beg of chart to single arrow, work single arrow to single arrow 7 times, work to end of chart. Follow the chart. Beg each row with ch 3. Work the last dc in the 3rd ch at beg of previous row. Fasten off. Work border around all edges by foll chart, sl st to join each round. Fasten off.

FINISHING
Pin piece to indicated measurement. Dampen and let dry. Cut pieces of star motif fabric 7" x 33" and 25¼" x 33". With right sides tog, sew the larger piece of blue lining fabric to the 33" wide edge of each piece of fabric, making a ¾" seam. Cut 2 pieces of fabric 23¼" x 33". Make a double seam on one 33" end of each piece of fabric. Overlap hemmed ends of pieces with right sides of both pieces up. Adjust pieces until tog they are the same size as the front piece. Sew side seams through both thicknesses. Place back and front of comforter cover with right sides tog and sew all seams. (To form rounded corner, cut out a circle in cardboard with a 5" diameter and place at corner. Trace around arc of circle at corner and sew along line. Turn right side out and sew ¼" seam around all edges.) Sew on the crochet border over lining fabric by hand.

KEY TO EDGING CHART
● = Ch st
T = Sc
Ŧ = Dc

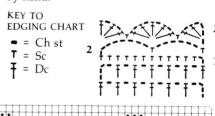

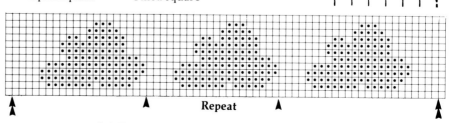

Repeat

BASSINETTE CURTAINS

See photo on page 97

SIZE
Curtain length: approx. 60¼" x 33¾".
Border approx. 5¾" wide.

MATERIALS
220 g crochet cotton thread. Steel crochet hook U.S. size 10. (U.K. size 4) 1 yd blue and white fabric with cloud motif 55" wide. 2 pieces of white cotton lining fabric 6¼" wide.

STITCHES USED
U.S. - Chain stitch (ch), single crochet (sc), double crochet (dc). U.K. - Chain stitch, double crochet, treble crochet.

GAUGE
26 squares in height and width = 4" x 4".

FILET CROCHET
Follow the chart. An open square = 1 dc, ch 1, skip 1 st of previous row, 1 dc. A filled square = 3 dc. On the chart, the last st of 1 square serves as the first st of the foll square.

DIRECTIONS
Ch 795 + ch 3 to turn (serves as first dc). Mark every 100th ch to use as a guide when counting.
ROW 1: 1 dc in the 6th ch from the hook, *ch 1, skip 1, 1 dc*, rep * to * across = 397 squares.
ROWS 2 to 33: For the side pieces, beg at right edge of chart, then work between the arrow 3 times, then work to end of chart (marked center) and work 2nd half to correspond. Beg each row with ch 3. Foll the chart. Work the last dc in the 3rd ch at beg of previous row.
ROWS 34 to 222: Work the first 33 squares only. Rep chart until piece measures desired length. Fasten off. Work the last 33 squares to correspond. Fasten off. Work border rows 1 - 3 of border chart.

FINISHING
Pin piece to indicated measurement. Dampen and let dry. Cut a piece of fabric 51¾" x 31¼" high. Along long edges and lower edge, make a double hem ¼" wide. At upper edge, make a double hem 1" wide. ¼" below upper hem, make 2 seams spaced ¼" apart to form casing. Place crochet border on the edges of the fabric and sew in place, leaving the upper casing ends open. Place lining fabric on wrong side of crochet border and zigzag to crochet edges after turning in edges to inside.

BASSINETTE SKIRT

See photo on page 97

SIZE
Border approx. 3¼" wide x 4½ yds long.

MATERIALS
180 g crochet cotton thread. Steel crochet hook U.S. size 8. (U.K. size 3) 3 yds blue and white fabric with star motif 55" wide. 8 ft of velcro.

STITCHES USED
U.S. - Chain stitch (ch), single crochet (sc), double crochet (dc). U.K. - Chain stitch, double crochet, treble crochet.

GAUGE
24 squares in height and width = 4" x 4".

FILET CROCHET
Follow the chart. An open square = 1 dc, ch 1, skip 1 st of previous row, 1 dc. A filled square = 3 dc. On the chart, the last st of 1 square serves as the first st of the foll square.

DIRECTIONS
Ch 1924. Mark every 100th ch to use as a guide when counting.
ROW 1: 1 dc in the 6th ch from the hook, *ch 1, skip 1, 1 dc*, rep * to * across = 960 squares.
ROWS 2 to 18: Follow chart. Work the pattern repeat 20 times. Beg each row with ch 5, 1 dc in the 6th ch from the hook. Work the last dc in the 3rd ch at beg of previous row. Fasten off. Work border rows 1 - 3 of border chart. Fasten off.

FINISHING
Pin piece to indicated measurement. Dampen and let dry. Cut 2 pieces of fabric 55" wide x 25½" high and a third piece 52" wide x 25½" high. Sew 2 seams ¾" along the 25½" edge with right sides tog so that you have a long piece 158" long. Along the long lower edge, make a double seam ¼" wide. Sew on the crochet border 4¼" from the lower edge at the single crochet rows of the

KEY TO CHART
□ = Open square   ● = Filled square

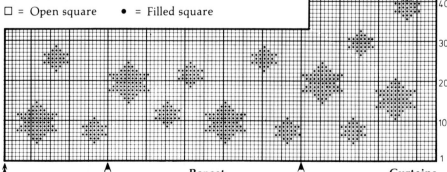

Center ⬆   ⬆   Repeat   ⬆   Curtains

borders. Zigzag stitch along the upper edge. Run a basting thread ¼" from upper edge. Make a double hem at the shorter ends and sew on strip of velcro on 1 side and pieces of velcro on the opposite side spaced ¼" from the upper edge to correspond. For the bassinette lining, cut 2 pieces of fabric 50¾" long x 15¾" wide. Sew the pieces tog at short ends right sides tog with a ¾" seam allowance. Along 1 long edge, make a double seam ¼" wide. Along the other long edge, gather to fit the skirt piece and with right sides tog, make a ¾" seam. Turn right side out and sew over gathered edge of skirt ¼" from seam. Sew the back seam of the lining with right sides tog and a ¾" seam, leaving a 1¼" space in the seam for the post for the curtain. Place lining over the bassinette and mark position of darts where needed to fit around curved edges. Remove lining and sew darts.

See chart on page 49, left column

BABY HEART VALANCE

See photo on page 98, top

SIZE
Approx. 11¾" high.

MATERIALS
100 g crochet cotton thread. Steel crochet hook U.S. size 6. (U.K. size 2)

STITCHES USED
U.S. - Chain stitch (ch), single crochet (sc), double crochet (dc). U.K. - Chain stitch, double crochet, treble crochet.

GAUGE
11½" squares x 12½ rows = 4" x 4".

FILET CROCHET
Follow the chart, which is worked sideways. An open square = 1 dc, ch 2, skip 2 sts of previous row, 1 dc. A filled square = 4 dc. On the chart, the last st of 1 square serves as the first st of the foll square.

DIRECTIONS
For a valance 9 points long, ch 82 + ch 3 (which serves as the first dc).
ROW 1: 1 dc in the 5th ch from the hook, 1 dc in each of the foll 2 ch, *ch 2, skip 2 ch, 1 dc in the foll ch*, work * to * twice, 1 dc in each of the foll 18 ch, work * to * 7 times, 1 dc in each of the foll 3 ch, work * to * 8 times, 1 dc in each of the foll 3 ch, ch 2, skip 2, 1 dc in the last ch. Turn. Continue by foll chart. Beg each row which beg with a filled square with ch 3. Beg each row which beg with an

open square with ch 5. Work inc and dec by foll chart. Work rep of chart. When 9 points have been completed, fasten off. Along the upper edge, make hangers as foll: 1 sc in the corner square, *ch 20, 1 sc in the same square, 2 sc in each of the foll 3 squares, 1 sc in the foll square*, rep * to * across, end with ch 20, 1 sc in the corner square. Fasten off.

FINISHING
Pin piece to indicated measurement. Dampen and let dry.

BABY HEART COVERLET

See photo on page 98, bottom

SIZE
Approx. 52" x 33".

MATERIALS
460 g crochet cotton thread. Steel crochet hook U.S. size 6. (U.K. size 2)

STITCHES USED
U.S. - Chain stitch (ch), slip stitch (sl st), single crochet (sc), double crochet (dc). U.K. - Chain stitch, slip stitch, double crochet, treble crochet.

GAUGE
11½" squares x 12½ rows = 4" x 4".

FILET CROCHET
Follow the chart, which is worked sideways. An open square = 1 dc, ch 2, skip 2 sts of previous row, 1 dc. A filled square = 4 dc. On the chart, the last st

of 1 square serves as the first st of the foll square.

DIRECTIONS
Ch 43 + ch 5 (which serves as the first dc).
ROW 1: 1 dc in the 8th ch from the hook, *ch 2, skip 2 ch, 1 dc in the foll ch*, work * to * 13 times. Turn.
ROW 2: Ch 5, skip 2 ch, 1 dc in each of the foll 7 dc, work * to * 8 times, 1 dc in each of the foll 6 dc, ch 2, skip 2, 1 dc in the last dc. Work by foll chart, beg each row with ch 5 for first open square. When chart is complete, fasten off. Make 77 heart motifs.

FINISHING
Pin the heart motifs to indicated measurements, dampen and let dry. Place the heart motifs 7 across and 11 down with center hearts pointing vertically. Join the squares by inserting hook through the first open square of 1 heart motif, and through the corresponding square of a 2nd heart motif, work 2 sc in each square. Continue by working 2 sc in each square across 7 heart motifs. Fasten off. Continue by joining heart motifs horizontally until there are 11 horizontal rows and join the heart motifs vertically in the same way. Work around the joined squares by inserting hook in the corner of 1 square and work 2 sc in the corner square, 2 sc in each of the foll squares and 5 sc in each corner, ending with 3 sc in the first corner. Slip stitch to join to first st. Fasten off.

Valance

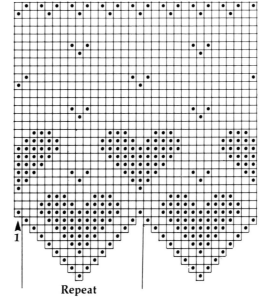

Repeat

BABY HEART:
Coverlet
Pillow
Pin Cushion

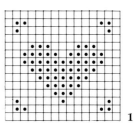

1

KEY TO CHARTS
☐ = Open square
● = Filled square

BABY HEART PILLOW

See photo on page 99 A

SIZE
Approx. 11" x 11".

MATERIALS
50 g crochet cotton thread for each pillow. Fabric 21¼" x 10½". Striped fabric 4¾" x 35½". Fiberfill stuffing. Satin ribbon 50" long, 1/3" wide. Steel crochet hook U.S. size 6. (U.K. size 2)

STITCHES USED
U.S. - Chain stitch (ch), slip stitch (sl st), single crochet (sc), double crochet (dc). U.K. - Chain stitch, slip stitch, double crochet, treble crochet.

GAUGE
11½ squares x 12½ rows = 4" x 4".

FILET CROCHET
Follow the chart, which is worked sideways. An open square = 1 dc, ch 2, skip 2 sts of previous row, 1 dc. A filled square = 4 dc. On the chart, the last st of 1 square serves as the first st of the foll square.

DIRECTIONS
Ch 43 + ch 5 (which serves as the first dc).
ROW 1: 1 dc in the 8th ch from the hook, *ch 2, skip 2 ch, 1 dc in the foll ch*, work * to * 13 times. Turn.
ROW 2: Ch 5, skip 2 ch, 1 dc in each of the foll 7 dc, work * to * 8 times, 1 dc in each of the foll 6 dc, ch 2, skip 2, 1 dc in the last dc. Work by foll chart, beg each row with ch 5 for first open square. When chart is complete, fasten off. Make 4 heart motifs.

FINISHING
Pin the heart motifs to indicated measurements, dampen and let dry. Place the heart motifs 2 across and 2 down with hearts pointing vertically. Join the squares by inserting hook through the first open square of 1 heart motif, and through the corresponding square of a 2nd heart motif, work 2 sc in each square until 2 squares are joined. Fasten off. Continue by joining heart motifs horizontally in the same manner.

Work around the joined squares by inserting hook in the corner of 1 square and work 2 sc, 2 sc in each of the foll squares and 5 sc in each corner, ending with 3 sc in the first corner. Slip stitch to join to first st. Fasten off. With right sides tog, sew the ends of striped fabric, fold with wrong sides tog and press fold.

Cut 2 pieces of fabric 10½" x 10½". Along the outside edges of the right side of 1 piece, place the striped ruffle around edges, gathering to fit. Pin in place and sew ¼" from edges. Place the other piece of fabric right sides tog on top of the first piece of fabric. Sew around the 3 sides of fabric ½" from the edges. Turn right side out. Sew on the filet piece to top of pillow. Stuff pillow and sew 4th side closed. Thread ribbon through outside rows of filet piece and tie in bow at 1 corner.

See chart on page 109

BABY HEART PIN CUSHION

See photo on page 99 B

SIZE
Approx. 5½" x 5½".

MATERIALS
15 g crochet cotton thread. Fabric 6" x 12". Striped fabric 1½" x 35½". Fiberfill stuffing. Satin ribbon 27½" long and 1/3" wide. Steel crochet hook U.S. size 6. (U.K. size 2)

STITCHES USED
U.S. - Chain stitch (ch), slip stitch (sl st), single crochet (sc), double crochet (dc). U.K. - Chain stitch, slip stitch, double crochet, treble crochet.

GAUGE
11½ squares x 12½ rows = 4" x 4".

FILET CROCHET
Follow the chart, which is worked sideways. An open square = 1 dc, ch 2, skip 2 sts of previous row, 1 dc. A filled square = 4 dc. On the chart, the last st of 1 square serves as the first st of the foll square.

DIRECTIONS
Ch 43 + ch 5 (which serves as the first dc).
ROW 1: 1 dc in the 8th ch from the hook, *ch 2, skip 2 ch, 1 dc in the foll ch*, work * to * 13 times. Turn.
ROW 2: Ch 5, skip 2 ch, 1 dc in each of the foll 7 dc, work * to * 8 times, 1 dc in each of the foll 6 dc, ch 2, skip 2, 1 dc in the last dc. Work by foll chart, beg each row with ch 5 for first open square. When chart is complete, fasten off.

FINISHING
Pin the heart motif to indicated measurements, dampen and let dry. Work around the square by inserting hook in the corner of square and work 2 sc, 2 sc in each of the foll squares and

5 sc in each corner, ending with 3 sc in the first corner. Slip stitch to join to first st. Fasten off. With right sides tog, sew the ends of striped fabric, then fold with wrong sides tog and press fold. Cut 2 pieces of fabric 6" x 6". Along the outside edges of the right side of 1 piece, place the striped ruffle around edges, gathering to fit. Pin in place and sew ¼" from edges. Place the other piece of fabric right sides tog on top of the first piece of fabric. Sew around the 3 sides of fabric ½" from the edges. Turn right side out. Sew on the filet piece to top of pillow. Stuff pillow and sew 4th side closed. Thread ribbon through outside rows of filet piece and tie in bow at 1 corner.

See chart on page 109

BABY BLANKET

See photo on page 100

SIZE
Each band is 6" wide and 51¼" long. The total is 35½" and total length is 51¼".

MATERIALS
650 g fingering weight cotton yarn. Steel crochet hook U.S. size 3. (U.K. size 1/0)

STITCHES USED
U.S. - Chain stitch (ch), slip stitch (sl st), double crochet (dc). U.K. - Chain stitch, slip stitch, treble crochet.

GAUGE
10 squares x 11 rows = 4".

FILET CROCHET
Follow the chart. An open square = 1 dc, ch 2, 1 dc. A filled square = 4 dc. On the chart, the last st of 1 square serves as the first st of the foll square. Work 3 bands beg at point A on chart and work 3 bands beg at point B.

DIRECTIONS
BAND A: Work by foll chart, beg with point A. Ch 46 + ch 3.
ROW 1: 1 dc in the 5th ch from the hook, 1 dc in the foll ch 2, *ch 2, skip 2 ch, 1 dc in the foll ch*, work * to * twice, 1 dc in each of the foll 12 ch, work * to * once, 1 dc in each of the foll 12 ch, work * to * twice, 1 dc in each of the foll 3 ch sts. Continue by working the chart. At the end of every row, turn and ch 3 for the first dc of the first filled square of ch 5 for the first open square. Work chart from points A to C 6 times, then work from point A to B once = 51¼" long. Fasten off. Make a total of 3 bands.

BAND B: Work by foll chart, beg with point B. ch 46 + ch 3.

ROW 1: 1 dc in the 9th ch from the hook, 1 dc in each of the foll 3 ch, *ch 2, skip 2 ch, 1 dc in the foll ch*, work * to * 5 times, 1 dc in each of the foll 3 ch, work * to * 5 times, 1 dc in each of the foll 3 ch, ch 2, skip 2 ch, 1 dc in the foll ch. Continue by foll chart. Work from point B to C once, then work from points A to C 6 times. Fasten off. Make a total of 3 bands.

FINISHING

Pin piece to indicated measurement. Dampen and let dry. Alternating bands A and B so that motifs are staggered, sew together by whipstitching together.

See chart on page 49, center column

BABY SHEET PANEL

See photo on page 101

See instructions and chart on page 49

LARGE PILLOW CASE

See photo on page 102

SIZE

Crochet square approx. 11" x 11". Pillow approx. 31½" x 31½" + 1½" border.

MATERIALS

150 g crochet cotton thread. Steel crochet hook U.S. size 6. (U.K. size 2) 35½" x 78½" white fabric.

STITCHES USED

U.S. - Chain stitch (ch), slip stitch (sl st), double crochet (dc). U.K. - Chain stitch, slip stitch, treble crochet.

GAUGE

16 squares in height and width = 4" x 4".

FILET CROCHET

Follow the chart.

DIRECTIONS

Ch 12 and sl st to join in a ring.
ROUND 1: Ch 3 (serves as first dc), 3 dc, *ch 5, 4 dc in ring*, rep * to * 3 times, ch 5, sl st to join to the 3rd ch of the turning ch. Continue by foll chart from rounds 2 to 21 (chart shows ¼ of square. Work other ¾ of square to correspond). Fasten off. Work 1 row of dc all around outside edges working 5 dc in each corner. Sl st to join. Fasten off. Make 4 squares.

FINISHING

Pin pieces to indicated measurement.

Dampen and let dry. Join the 4 squares with slip stitch. Work 1 round of dc around edges of large square working 5 dc in each corner. Make a ¼" double hem on each small end of fabric. Fold the fabric with right sides tog, overlapping ends so piece measures 21¼" square. Sew side seams. Turn right side out and sew through all thickness 1½" from each edge. Sew on filet crochet to center of pillow.

SMALL PILLOW CASE

See photo on page 102

SIZE

Crochet square approx. 11" x 11". Pillow approx. 15¾" x 15¾".

MATERIALS

50 g crochet cotton thread. Steel crochet hook U.S. size 6. (U.K. size 2) 19¾" x 47" white fabric.

STITCHES USED

U.S. - Chain stitch (ch), slip stitch (sl st), double crochet (dc). U.K. - Chain stitch, slip stitch, treble crochet.

GAUGE

16 squares in height and width = 4" x 4".

FILET CROCHET

Follow the chart.

DIRECTIONS

Ch 12 and sl st to join in a ring.
ROUND 1: Ch 3 (serves as first dc), 3 dc, *ch 5, 4 dc in ring*, rep * to * 3 times, ch 5, sl st to join to the 3rd ch of the turning ch. Continue by foll chart from rounds 2 to 21 (chart shows ¼ of square. Work other ¾ of square to correspond). Fasten off. Work 1 row of dc all around outside edges working 5 dc in each corner. Sl st to join. Fasten off.

FINISHING

Pin piece to indicated measurement. Dampen and let dry. Make ¼" double hem on each small end of fabric. Fold the fabric with right sides tog, overlapping ends so piece measures 13¼" square. Sew side seams. Turn right side out and sew through all thickness 1½" from each edge. Sew on filet crochet to center of pillow.

SHEET BORDER
PILLOW BORDER

See photo on page 103

SIZE

Width of sheet approx. 59". Pillow size approx. 31½" x 31½". Width of border approx. 2".

MATERIALS

50 g crochet cotton thread. Steel crochet hook U.S. size 8. (U.K. size 3) 1 sheet

KEY TO CHART
- = Ch
┼ = Dc
▲ = Sl st

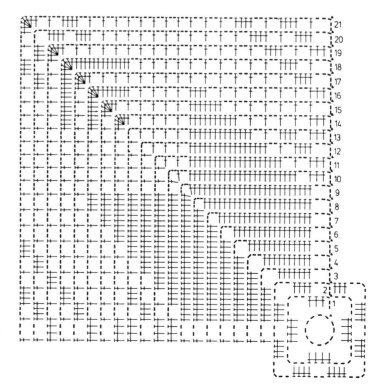

and pillow case. A piece of pink fabric the same width and length as the border.

STITCHES USED

U.S. - Chain stitch (ch), single crochet (sc), double crochet (dc). U.K. - Chain stitch, double crochet, treble crochet.

GAUGE

18 squares x 21 rows = 4" x 4".

FILET CROCHET

Follow the chart. An open square = 1 dc, ch 1, skip 1 sts of previous row, 1 dc. A filled square = 3 dc. On the chart, the last st of 1 square serves as the first st of the foll square.

DIRECTIONS

Ch 27 + ch 3 (serves as first dc).
ROW 1: 1 dc in the 4th ch from the hook, 1 dc in each of the foll ch = 28 dc. Continue by foll chart from rows 2 to 22, repeat rows 1 to 22 5 times, ending with rows 1 to 3 for the pillow borders. Make a 2nd border. Rep rows 1 to 22, 14 times, ending with rows 1 to 3 for the sheet. Beg each row with ch 3 and always work the last dc in the 3rd ch of the turning ch of previous row. Fasten off.

FINISHING

Pin pieces to indicated measurement. Dampen and let dry. The pillow pieces will measure 2" x 21¼". The sheet pieces will measure 2" x 58¼". Cut pieces of pink fabric the same size as filet pieces. Sew filet piece 5½" from the top of the pillow with pink fabric underneath, centering piece. Sew on a 2nd piece 1½" from the first. See photo. Sew sheet piece 6" from the top edge of the sheet.

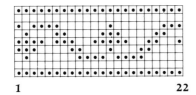

1   22

KEY TO CHART

□ = Open square   ● = Filled square

ROSE MOTIF PILLOW

See photo on page 104, A

SIZE

5" x 24 ½" filet strip on 15¾" x 23½" pillow.

MATERIALS

30 g crochet cotton thread. Steel crochet hook U.S. size 14. (U.K. size 6) Polished cotton fabric 24½" x 41". Light blue satin 5" x 24½". Light blue satin ribbon 1" wide x 49" long.

STITCHES USED

U.S. - Chain stitch (ch), slip stitch (sl st), double crochet (dc). U.K. - Chain stitch, slip stitch, treble crochet.

GAUGE

24 squares in height and width = 4" x 4".

FILET CROCHET

Follow the chart. An open square = 1 dc, ch 1, skip 1 st of previous row, 1 dc. A filled square = 3 dc. On the chart, the last st of 1 square serves as the first st of the foll square.

DIRECTIONS

Ch 98. 1 dc in 8th ch from hook. Continue by foll chart: *ch 1, skip 1, 1 dc in the foll ch*, rep * to * across = 31 squares. Beg each row with ch 7, skip first ch of previous row and insert hook in first dc, work across by foll chart. Rep rows 1 to 28 of chart until piece measures approx. 24½" = 5 rose motifs. Fasten off.

FINISHING

Pin piece to indicated measurement (5" x 24½"). Dampen and let dry. Make a ¾" hem on the narrow ends of the cotton fabric. On the right side of work, spaced 13" from one end, sew on blue satin band and sew on crochet band over blue satin band. Sew ribbons over the edges of the crocheted band. Fold fabric, right sides tog, overlapping ends by 6¼". With right sides tog, sew side seams, sewing through all thicknesses at ribbon and crocheted band. See photo. Turn right side out. Sew lower and upper edges for ¼".

ROSE MOTIF PILLOW

See photo on page 104, B

SIZE

4¾" x 24½" filet strip on 15¾" x 23½" pillow.

MATERIALS

30 g crochet cotton thread. Steel crochet hook U.S. size 14. (U.K. size 6) Polished cotton fabric 24½" x 41". Light blue satin 6" x 24½". Light blue satin ribbon ½" wide x 49" long.

STITCHES USED

U.S. - Chain stitch (ch), double crochet (dc). U.K. - Chain stitch, treble crochet.

GAUGE

24 squares in height and width = 4" x 4".

FILET CROCHET

Follow the chart. An open square = 1 dc, ch 1, skip 1 st of previous row, 1 dc. A filled square = 3 dc. On the chart, the last st of 1 square serves as the first st of the foll square.

DIRECTIONS

Ch 89. Work 1 dc in 4th ch from hook, continue by foll chart for row 1. Work rows 2 to 30, then rep rows 1 to 30 of chart until piece measures approx. 24½" = 5 rose motifs. Fasten off.

FINISHING

Pin piece to indicated measurement (4¾" x 24½"). Dampen and let dry. Make a ¾" hem on the narrow ends of the cotton fabric. Fold under long edges of satin band and iron so that satin band measures 4¾" wide. On the right side of work, spaced 13" from one end, sew on blue satin band and sew on crochet band over blue satin band. Sew on 2 ribbons spaced ¼" and 1¼" apart. Fold fabric, right sides tog, overlapping ends by 6¼". With wrong sides tog, sew side seams, sewing through all thicknesses at ribbon and crocheted band. See photo. Turn right side out. Sew lower and upper edges for ¼".

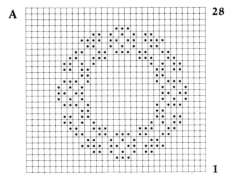

A   28

1

KEY TO CHARTS

□ = Open square   ● = Filled square

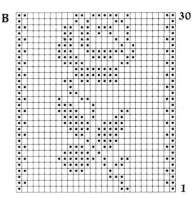

B   30

1

TABLECLOTHS AND RUNNERS

T able tops are an ideal place to showcase your filet crochet handwork. Tablecloths of filet crochet drape beautifully over all shapes of tables, and they can be rotated

TABLECLOTHS AND RUNNERS

at different angles to produce a multitude of effects.

As shown on the **previous page**, *filet crochet tablecloths can complement even the most formal center-pieces, such as a silver tea service. (see page 129 for directions) The designer chose a traditional windmill motif and mixes it with a zigzag motif that follows the shape of her tablecloth.*

Left, *a filet tablecloth with flower and trellis motifs looks light and summery over a yellow linen cloth. (see page 129 for directions)*

Right, *a cascade of roses decorates the sides and top of this filet tablecloth. (see page 130 for directions)*

TABLECLOTHS AND RUNNERS

A white linen table cloth edged with filet crochet makes an elegant touch for a summer garden party. (see page 130 for directions)

In many parts of Europe, formal tablecloths are accented with openwork and double hems with mitered corners before adding a filet edging. Should the tablecloth ever become stained or start to yellow, simply remove the filet edging and use it to create something new.

This tablecloth also makes an easy transition to a small corner table in a bedroom or den.

TABLECLOTHS AND RUNNERS

*O*utdoor entertaining is easy and elegant when you top an ordinary table with a tablecloth edged with filet crochet.

Opposite page, contemporary geometrical motifs combine with a traditional snowflake pattern to form an eye-catching edging. (see page 133 for directions) The rickrack edge is simple to make and echoes the geometric motifs in the filet.

Right, a small, double-hemmed tablecloth is decorated with a filet edging with a repeating flower motif (see page 131 for directions). A portion of the zigzag hem serves as a flower pot for each flower.

TABLECLOTHS AND RUNNERS

T*he scalloped edges of this filet tablecloth enhance the delicacy of the center- piece bowl filled with fresh roses and baby's breath. (see page 133 for directions)*

The art nouveau floral motifs blend with both contemporary and traditional decors, and you can change the color of the undercloth to further increase design possibilities.

TABLECLOTHS AND RUNNERS

Opposite page, a single bouquet of tulips in each of the tablecloth's four corners forms a simple, elegant look that complements even the finest crystal.

(see page 134 for directions) For evening entertaining, the traditional linen undercloth is replaced with one of shimmering peach satin.

Below, a star motif filet edging adds charm to an everyday tablecloth. (see page 134 for directions) Note how well the filet blends with a yellow checked fabric,

and how the filet edging is pleated in the corners of the tablecloth for a professional finish.

TABLECLOTHS AND RUNNERS

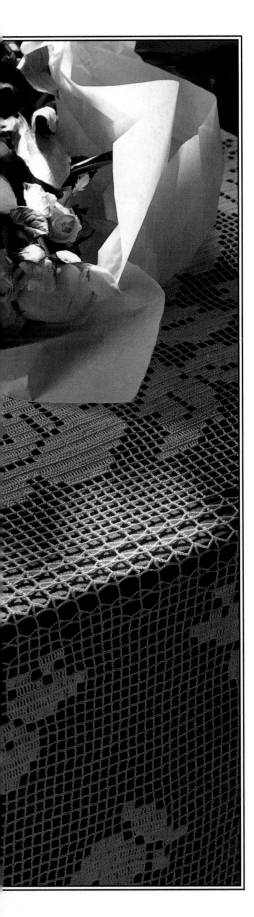

Thislarge filet crochet tablecloth, **left**, celebrates a passion for roses. (see page 136 for directions) The center bouquet of roses is bordered with filet openwork, and the sides of the cloth feature scalloped garlands of rose buds.

Below, create a more casual look with a filet-edged tablecloth by adding a row of fringe to the bottom edges. (see page 136 for directions)

TABLECLOTHS AND RUNNERS

Filet crochet is as stylish on a table at a vacation beach house as it is on a formal table. The tablecloth shown here is made by crocheting the entire cloth in open filet squares first, and then adding the stripes one color at a time with a larger hook. (see page 137 for directions)

Matching pillows, curtains, and other accessories are also simple to make. Just continue making open filet squares until your piece is the desired size and then add the stripes.

TABLECLOTHS AND RUNNERS

Many of the motifs in this book can also be used to adorn tables of all lengths and widths. A table runner with elaborate edges, like the one shown here, is a challenge to make but well worth the effort (see page 138 for directions) Note how clever use of openwork and how the edging design follows the outer border's filet motif.

Table runners can also double as bedroom accents by laying them across the bottom of a bedspread.

TABLECLOTH

See photo on page 113

SIZE

Approx. 23½" x 23½".

MATERIALS

150 g crochet cotton thread. Steel crochet hook U.S. size 8. (U.K. size 3)

STITCHES USED

U.S. - Chain stitch (ch), triple crochet (tr). U.K. - Chain stitch, double treble crochet.

GAUGE

12 squares in height and width = 4" x 4".

FILET CROCHET

Follow the chart. An open square = 1 tr, ch 3, skip 3 sts of previous row, 1 tr. A filled square = 5 tr. On the chart, the last st of 1 square serves as the first st of the foll square.

DIRECTIONS

Ch 8.

ROW 1: Insert hook in the 5th ch from hook, work 1 tr in the following 3 ch = 5 tr. Continue by foll chart. Work increases and decreases as shown on chart. Inc at beg of row: ch 8. Work first tr in the 5th, 6th, 7th, and 8th ch from the hook. 1 inc square at the end of the row: ch 3, then wrap yarn around the hook twice, insert hook in the last tr of the previous row, *yo and draw through 2 loops*, rep * to * until 1 loop remains. Decreases: at beg of row, sl st over desired number of dec sts. At end of row, leave desired number of dec squares unworked. When chart is complete, fasten off.

FINISHING

Pin piece to indicated measurement. Dampen and let dry.

TABLECLOTH

See photo on page 114

SIZE

Approx. 41¾" x 41¾".

MATERIALS

400 g crochet cotton thread. Steel crochet hook U.S. size 8. (U.K. size 3)

STITCHES USED

U.S. - Chain stitch (ch), triple crochet (tr). U.K. - Chain stitch, double treble crochet.

GAUGE

12 squares in height and width = 4" x 4".

FILET CROCHET

Follow the chart. An open square = 1 tr, ch 3, skip 3 sts of previous row, 1 tr. A filled square = 5 tr. On the chart, the last st of 1 square serves as the first st of the foll square.

DIRECTIONS

Ch 508 + ch 4 to turn.

ROW 1: Tr in the 5th ch from hook, tr in each foll ch = 509 tr. Continue by foll chart, work row 2 to 64, then for 2nd half work rows 63 to 1. Beg each row with ch 4 and work last tr in the last ch of turning row. Fasten off.

FINISHING

Pin piece to indicated measurement. Dampen and let dry.

See chart on page 130

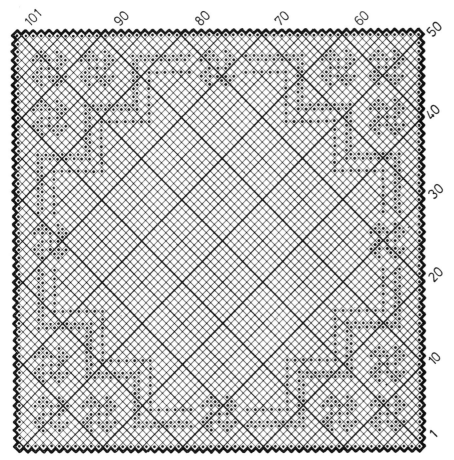

KEY TO CHART

☐ = Open square   • = Filled square

See photo on page 113

Both American and British stitches are listed under STITCHES USED in each pattern, however, only the American terms are used in the text. British readers should convert these instructions to British terms as they work the projects.

TABLECLOTH
See photo on page 115

SIZE
Approx. 43¼" x 43¼".

MATERIALS
500 g crochet cotton thread. Steel crochet hook U.S. size 8. (U.K. size 3)

STITCHES USED
U.S. - Chain stitch (ch), triple crochet (tr). U.K. - Chain stitch, double treble crochet.

GAUGE
12 squares in height and width = 4" x 4".

FILET CROCHET
Follow the chart. An open square = 1 tr, ch 3, skip 3 sts of previous row, 1 tr. A filled square = 5 tr. On the chart, the last st of 1 square serves as the first st of the foll square.

DIRECTIONS
Ch 536 + ch 4 to turn (serves as first tr). Mark every 50th ch st with a strand of a different color yarn to use as a guide when counting.
ROW 1: 1 tr in the 5th ch from the hook, 1 tr in each ch across = 537 tr. Continue by foll chart from rows 2 to 67, then

work from row 67 to 1. Beg each row with ch 4 and always work the last tr in the 4th ch of the turning ch of previous row. Fasten off.

FINISHING
Pin piece to indicated measurement. Dampen and let dry.

TABLECLOTH
See photo on page 116

SIZE
Approx. 55" x 55".

MATERIALS
190 g crochet cotton thread. Steel crochet hook U.S. size 10. (U.K. size 4) Linen fabric about 51¼" x 51¼".

STITCHES USED
U.S. - Chain stitch (ch), slip stitch (sl st), double crochet (dc). U.K. - Chain stitch, slip stitch, treble crochet.

GAUGE
27 squares wide = 6". 32 rows = 4".

FILET CROCHET
Follow the chart. An open square = 1 dc, ch 2, skip 2 sts of previous row, 1 dc. A

filled square = 4 dc. On the chart, the last st of 1 square serves as the first st of the foll square.

DIRECTIONS
FIRST SIDE
Ch 105 + ch 3 to turn.
ROW 1: 1 dc in the 4th through the 9th ch from the hook (= 2 filled squares), continue by foll chart, working increases and decreases as shown on chart. Work rows 1 to 92. Work rows 9 to 92, 3 times. End with rows 93 to 134, working each arc separately. Beg each even row with ch 3 and work the last dc in the 3rd ch of the turning ch of the previous row.
Turn work and beg row 1 of 2nd side by joining thread to end of row 133 with a slip st (see arrow on chart). Work rem sides the same, then sew the 4th side to the first side with very fine sts. Work last round of ch and dc by foll edging chart. Fasten off.

FINISHING
Pin piece to indicated measurement. Dampen and let dry. Cut the fabric to correspond to the finished measurement of the border, allowing 6" for double hem. Make a 2" double hem with mitered corners, then work openwork row by gathering 3 threads tog, each

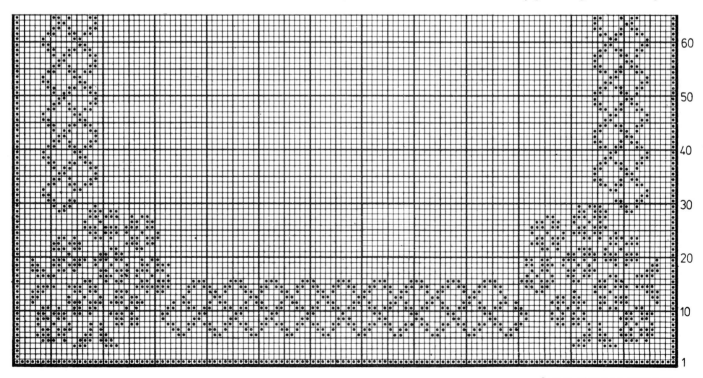

KEY TO CHART
☐ = Open square
● = Filled square

Instructions on page 129
Photo on page 114

hole separated by 3 threads. See photo.
(Instructions for double hem, mitered
corners and openwork can be found in
General Instructions at front of book.)

See chart on page 132

TABLECLOTH
See photo on page 118

SIZE
Approx. 39¼" x 39¼".

MATERIALS
120 g crochet cotton thread. Steel
crochet hook U.S. size 10. (U.K. size 4)
Linen fabric about 45¼" x 45¼".

STITCHES USED
U.S. - Chain stitch (ch), slip stitch (sl st),
double crochet (dc). U.K. - Chain stitch,
slip stitch, treble crochet.

GAUGE
27 squares wide = 4". 16 rows = 2".

FILET CROCHET
Follow the chart. An open square = 1 dc,
ch 2, skip 2 sts of previous row, 1 dc. A
filled square = 4 dc. On the chart, the
last st of 1 square serves as the first st
of the foll square.

DIRECTIONS
FIRST SIDE
Ch 72. Beg with row 1 of chart. 1 dc in
the 4th to the 9th ch from the hook
(= 2 filled squares), continue by foll
chart, working increases and decreases
as shown on chart. Work rows 1 to 16,
15 times, end with rows 17 to 62. Beg
each even row with ch 3 and work the
last dc in the 3rd ch of the turning ch of
the previous row.
Turn work and beg row 1 of 2nd side by
joining thread to end of row 29 (as
indicated by arrow on chart) with a sl st.
Work the first row along upper edge of
previous piece, evenly spacing sts. Work
same as the first side, then work rem
sides the same, then sew the 4th side to
the first side with very fine sts. Work
last round of ch and dc of edging chart.
Fasten off.

FINISHING
Pin piece to indicated measurement.
Dampen and let dry. Cut the fabric to
correspond to the finished measurement
of the border, allowing 4" for hem.
Make a double 2" hem with mitered
corners, then work openwork row by
gathering 3 threads tog, each hole

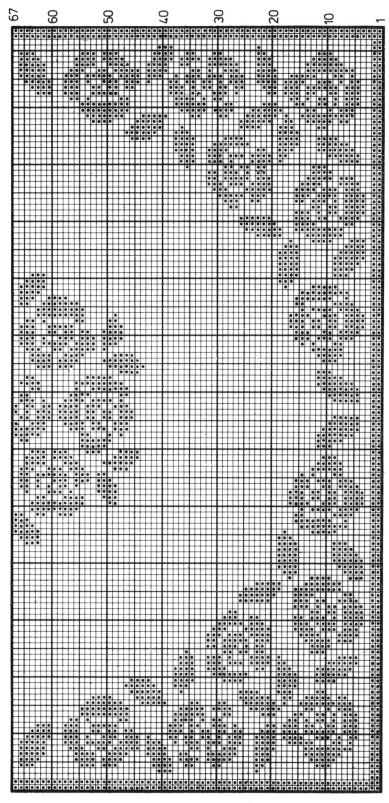

Instructions on page 130
Photo on page 115

KEY TO CHART
□ = Open square
● = Filled square

131

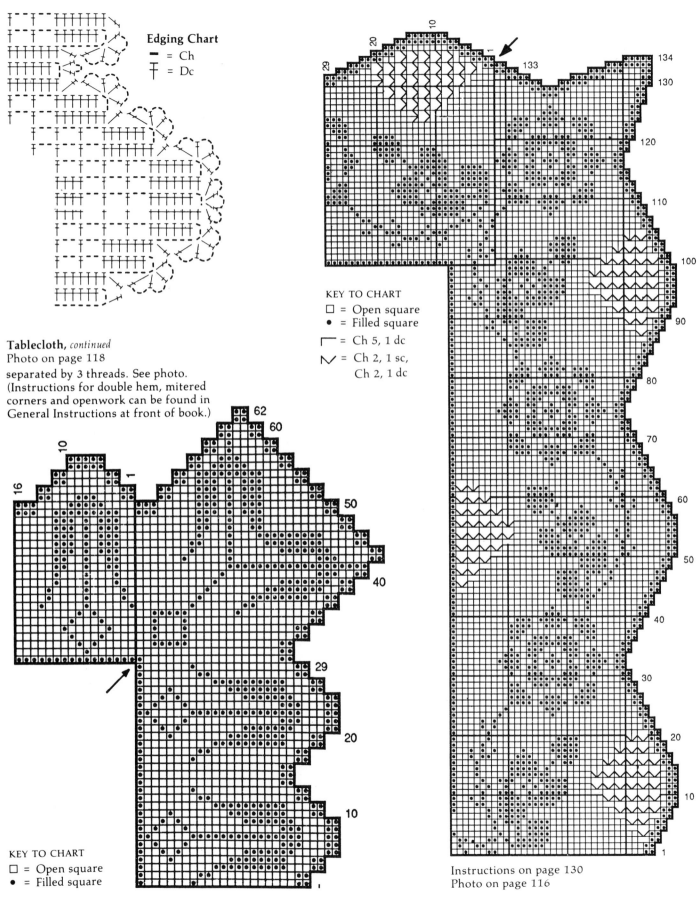

Edging Chart
— = Ch
‡ = Dc

KEY TO CHART
□ = Open square
• = Filled square
⌐ = Ch 5, 1 dc
∨ = Ch 2, 1 sc,
Ch 2, 1 dc

Tablecloth, *continued*
Photo on page 118

separated by 3 threads. See photo.
(Instructions for double hem, mitered
corners and openwork can be found in
General Instructions at front of book.)

KEY TO CHART
□ = Open square
• = Filled square

Instructions on page 130
Photo on page 116

TABLECLOTH

See photo on page 119

SIZE
Approx. 43¼" x 43¼".

MATERIALS
150 g crochet cotton thread. Steel crochet hook U.S. size 8. (U.K. size 3) Linen fabric about 45¼" x 45¼".

STITCHES USED
U.S. - Chain stitch (ch), slip stitch (sl st), double crochet (dc). U.K. - Chain stitch, slip stitch, treble crochet.

GAUGE
24 squares wide = 3¼".
24 rows long = 3 1/3".

FILET CROCHET
Follow the chart. An open square = 1 dc, ch 2, skip 2 sts of previous row, 1 dc. A filled square = 4 dc. On the chart, the last st of 1 square serves as the first st of the foll square.

DIRECTIONS

FIRST SIDE
Ch 67. Beg with row 18 of chart as foll:
ROW 18: 1 dc in the 9th, 10th, 11th and 12th ch from the hook (= 1 filled square), continue by foll chart, working increases and decreases as shown on chart. Work rows 18 to 24. Work rows 1 to 24, 10 times. End with rows 25 to 43. Turn work and beg row 18 of 2nd side by joining thread to end of last row 20 (as indicated by arrow on chart) with a slip st. You will be working across top of first piece. Evenly distribute sts from 20th to 38th row. Work same as the first side, then work rem sides the same. Sew the 4th side end to the first side of beg row with very fine sts. Work last round of ch and dc by foll edging chart. Fasten off.

FINISHING
Pin piece to indicated measurement. Dampen and let dry. Cut the fabric to correspond to the finished measurement of the border, allowing 4" for hem. Make a 2" double hem with mitered corners, then work openwork row and corners by gathering 3 threads tog, each hole separated by 3 threads. See photo. (Instructions for double hem, mitered corners, and openwork can be found in General Instructions at front of book.)

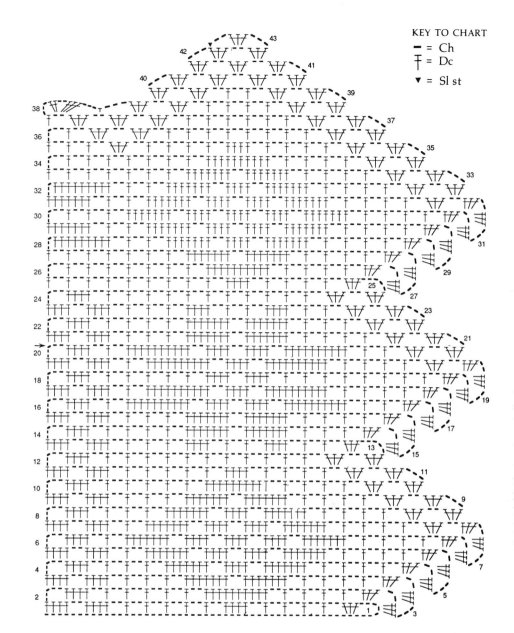

KEY TO CHART
- = Ch
⊤ = Dc
▼ = Sl st

TABLECLOTH

See photo on page 120

SIZE
43¼" round.

MATERIALS
340 g crochet cotton. Steel crochet hook U.S. size 8. (U.K. size 3)

STITCHES USED
U.S. - Chain stitch (ch), slip stitch (sl st), double crochet (dc). U.K. - Chain stitch, slip stitch, treble crochet.

GAUGE
22 squares = 4".

FILET CROCHET
Follow the chart. An open square = 1 dc, ch 1, skip 1 st of previous row, 1 dc. A filled square = 3 dc. On the chart, the last st of 1 square serves as the first st of the foll square.

INCREASES AT THE BEG OF A ROW
Ch 2 for the lower edge of every open square you wish to increase, plus ch 4 which will serve as the first dc. Work the first dc in the 7th ch from the hook.

Example: to inc 3 open squares, ch 6 + ch 4 = ch 10.

INCREASES AT THE END OF A ROW

To inc 1 open square, work as foll: ch 1, wrap yarn around hook 3 times, insert hook under the last worked dc, yo, then *yo, draw through 2 loops on hook*, work * to * 4 times = 1 filled square. For an open square, work * to * twice.

DECREASES AT THE BEG OF A ROW

Sl st across the sts of the sts you wish to decrease.

DECREASES AT THE END OF A ROW

Leave the squares you wish to decrease unworked.

DIRECTIONS

Work by foll chart, beg with scallop A. Ch 23 for lower edge + ch 4. Work 11 open squares, work the first dc in the 7th ch from the hook. Turn and inc 4 open squares at beg of foll row, work 11 open squares, inc 4 open squares at the end of 2nd row = 19 open squares. In the 3rd row, inc 3 open squares at each end and work 11 filled squares (= 23 dc at center). Work scallop A to the 15 row, ending this row with ch 4. Break yarn. Work scallop B. Ch 21 + ch 4. Work the first dc in the 7th ch from the hook = 10 open squares. Work to the 8th row by foll chart, then sl st to join to the 4th ch of scallop A. Break yarn. Work scallop C. Ch 21 + ch 4. Work by foll chart (reverse of scallop B. Beg at left edge so as to reverse shaping and motif). End row 8 with ch 4 and sl st to the top of the first st of the 15th row of scallop A. Break yarn. Join a new yarn at the edge of scallop B. Work over the 3 scallops by foll the chart, inc open squares as required. Work to center of chart (= M), then work the 2nd half by rev chart.

FINISHING

Work 1 round of dc around all edges, working 2 dc in each open square and 3 dc in the corner squares. Pin piece to indicated measurement forming a circle. Dampen and let dry.

See chart on page 135

TABLECLOTH
See photo on page 122

SIZE

Tablecloth: about 55" wide and 55" long. Filet border: 4½" wide.

MATERIALS

190 g crochet cotton thread. Steel crochet hook U.S. size 12. (U.K. size 5) Woven cotton fabric 55" x 55".

STITCHES USED

U.S. - Chain stitch (ch), single crochet (sc), double crochet (dc). U.K. - Chain stitch, double crochet, treble crochet.

GAUGE

18 squares x 28 rows = 4" x 4".

FILET CROCHET

Follow the chart. An open square = 1 dc, ch 2, skip 2 sts of previous row, 1 dc. A filled square = 4 dc. Squares with V's = 1 dc, ch 2, 1 sc under the ch 2 of previous row, ch 2. On the chart, the last st of 1 square serves as the first st of the foll square.

DIRECTIONS

Ch 52 + ch 3 to turn (serves as first dc). ROW 1: 1 dc in the 4th ch from the hook, then foll the chart. Each row beg with ch 3 which counts as the first dc. Work

Rows 2 to 33 until you have 52 star motifs. Fasten off.

FINISHING

Pin piece to indicated measurement. Dampen and let dry. Make a double hem with mitered corners all around fabric. Sew on border with 1 star at each corner, pleated to fit at corner. See photo.

See chart on page 48, center column

TULIP TABLECLOTH
See photo on page 123

SIZE

Approx. 47¼" x 47¼".

MATERIALS

500 g crochet cotton thread. Steel crochet hook U.S. size 8. (U.K. size 3)

STITCHES USED

U.S. - Chain stitch (ch), double crochet (dc). U.K. - Chain stitch, treble crochet.

↑ Center

KEY TO CHART

☐ = Open square   • = Filled square

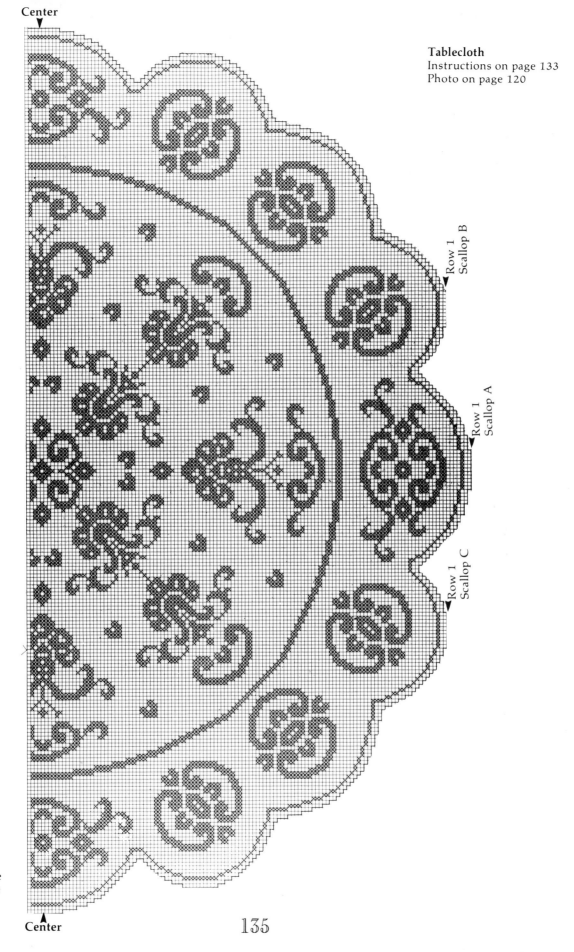

Tablecloth
Instructions on page 133
Photo on page 120

Row 1
Scallop B

Row 1
Scallop A

Row 1
Scallop C

KEY TO CHART
☐ = Open square
x = Filled square

GAUGE

15 squares in height and width = 4" x 4".

FILET CROCHET

Follow the chart. An open square = 1 dc, ch 2, skip 2 sts of previous row, 1 dc. A filled square = 4 dc. On the chart, the last st of 1 square serves as the first st of the foll square.

DIRECTIONS

Ch 540 + ch 3 to turn (serves as first dc). Mark every 50th ch st with a strand of a different color yarn to use as a guide in counting.
ROW 1: 1 dc in the 4th ch from the hook, 1 dc in each ch across = 541 dc. Continue by foll chart, beg each row with ch 3, working the last dc of each row in the ch 3 of the previous row. Work rows 2 to 90 of chart, then rev by working row 90 to row 1 of chart. Fasten off.

FINISHING

Pin piece to indicated measurement. Dampen and let dry.

TABLECLOTH

See photo on page 124

See instructions for Floral Curtain on page 83

TABLECLOTH

See photo on page 125

SIZE
Edging approx. 6¼".

MATERIALS
1000 g crochet cotton thread. Steel crochet hook U.S. size 4. (U.K. size 1) Fabric 52" x 52".

STITCHES USED
U.S. - Chain stitch (ch), double crochet (dc). U.K. - Chain stitch, treble crochet.

GAUGE
15 squares in height and 12½ squares in width = 4" x 4".

FILET CROCHET
Follow the chart. An open square = 1 dc, ch 2, skip 2 sts of previous row, 1 dc. A filled square = 4 dc. On the chart, the last st of 1 square serves as the first st of the foll square.

DIRECTIONS
Worked in 4 strips, and the corners are

worked to join sides.
Ch 61 + ch 3 to turn (serves as first dc).
ROW 1: 1 dc in the 5th ch from the hook, 1 dc in each of the foll 2 ch, *ch 2, skip 2 ch, 1 dc in the foll ch (= 1 open square)*, work * to * 9 times, 1 dc in each of the foll 3 ch, work * to * 5 times, 1 dc in the foll 3 ch, work * to * twice, 1 dc in each of the foll 3 ch.
ROW 2: Ch 3, 1 dc in each of the foll 3 dc (= filled square), 3 open squares, 1 filled square, 8 open squares, 1 filled square, 6 open squares, end with 1 dc in top of ch 3 of turning ch, ch 3 to turn. Continue by foll chart, beg with ch 5 for the first open square and ch 3 for the first dc of a filled square. Work the pat rep 13 times or desired length, then work the rows on chart between rep and first row of corner. Fasten off. Make 3 more sides. Join at corners by working along the edge of the last row of 1 side, slip stitching over the last square and working along the first row of the next side as follows: ROW 1: Join thread to the right edge of the last row: Ch 3, 9 open squares, 1 filled square, 65 open squares, 1 filled square, 1 open square, sl st over the last square. In the last dc of the sl st square, work 1 dc, then work across the first row of a 2nd side. Work 1 open square, 1 filled square, 5 open squares, 1 filled square, 1 open square, 1 filled square, 9 open squares. ROW 2:

1 filled square, 9 open squares, 1 filled square, 5 open squares, 1 filled square, 1 open square, sl st over last square, and work along the side of the first edge by foll chart. Continue until chart is complete, then fasten off. Work rem 3 corners.

FINISHING
Pin piece to indicated measurement. Dampen and let dry. Along edges of fabric, make a ¼" hem and sew on border. Make fringe about 9½" long with 8 strands in each fringe. Fold fringe in half and knot along edges of borders through open squares at edges.

TEACOSY

See photo on page 125

SIZE
Approx. 9" high.

MATERIALS
100 g crochet cotton thread. Steel crochet hook U.S. size 4. (U.K. size 1)

STITCHES USED
U.S. - Chain stitch (ch), slip stitch (sl st), single crochet (sc), double crochet (dc). U.K. - Chain stitch, slip stitch, double crochet, treble crochet.

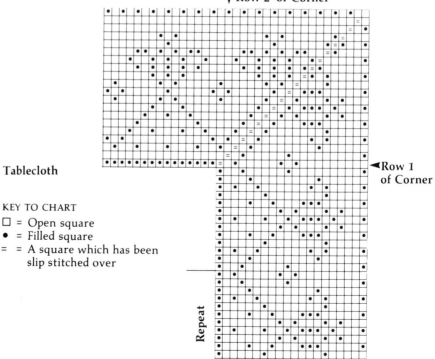

▼ Row 2 of Corner

◄ Row 1 of Corner

Tablecloth

KEY TO CHART
□ = Open square
● = Filled square
= = A square which has been slip stitched over

Repeat

◄ Row 1 of Border

GAUGE

15 squares in height and 12½ squares in width = 4" x 4".

FILET CROCHET

Follow the chart. An open square = 1 dc, ch 2, skip 2 sts of previous row, 1 dc. A filled square = 4 dc. On the chart, the last st of 1 square serves as the first st of the foll square.

DIRECTIONS

Worked in 2 pieces. Ch 142 + ch 5 to turn (serves as first open square).
ROW 1: 1 dc in the 8th ch from the hook, *ch 2, skip 2, 1 dc in the foll ch*, rep * to * across = 47 open squares. Continue by foll chart, beg with ch 5 for the first open square and ch 3 for the first dc of a filled square. Always work the last dc in the 3rd ch of the turning ch of previous row. Work decreases as shown on chart. Dec 1 open square at the beg of a row by sl stitching across 1 square, ch 3, work 1 dc in the foll dc, continue by foll chart. Dec 1 open square at the end of a row by leaving last square unworked, work 1 dc in the last dc. Fasten off. Make a 2nd piece. Along the lower edge of each piece work as foll: *1 sc in each square, 1 picot (ch 3, 1 sc in the 3rd ch from the hook)*, rep * to *, end with 1 sc.

FINISHING

Pin pieces to indicated measurement. Dampen and let dry. Place pieces right sides tog and sc around side and upper edges.

TABLECLOTH

See photo on page 126

SIZE

Approx. 32¾" x 39¼".

MATERIALS

500 g white crochet cotton thread. 10 g each of the following colors: yellow, blue, green and pink. Steel crochet hook U.S. size 4. (U.K. size 1) For stripes: Crochet hook U.S. size E/4 and H/8. (U.K. size 9 and 6)

STITCHES USED

U.S. - Chain stitch (ch), double crochet (dc). U.K. - Chain stitch, treble crochet.

GAUGE

16 squares in height and 14 squares in width = 4" x 4".

FILET CROCHET

An open square = 1 dc, ch 1, skip 1 st of previous row, 1 dc. The last st of 1 square serves as the first st of the foll square.

DIRECTIONS

Ch 323 + ch 4 to turn (serves as first open square).
ROW 1: 1 dc in the 7th ch from the hook, *ch 1, skip 1 ch, 1 dc*, rep * to * across = 161 open squares.
ROW 2: Ch 4, 1 dc in the foll dc, *ch 1, 1 dc in the foll dc*, rep * to *. Rep row 2 until you have 117 rows. Fasten off.

FINISHING

Pin piece to indicated measurement. Dampen and let dry. Stripes: with size H/8 hook, work vertical stripes: beg with the 4th open square from the right edge. With green thread under the filet piece (with 4" end overhanging edge), insert hook from top and draw through a green loop. Insert hook through foll open square and draw through loop then draw through loop on hook. Continue chaining thru open squares to opposite edge. Leave 4" end overhanging edge. Skip 10 open squares, work more stripes as foll: 1 each in blue, pink and yellow. Then rep colors, ending 3 open squares from the left side. Horizontal stripes: with size E/4 hook, beg with the 4th open square from the lower edge and work same as vertical stripes. Space 7 open squares between each stripe. Work colors in foll order: yellow, pink, blue and green. Work last stripe 3 open squares from edge. Cut 4 strands 8" long of each color for each fringe. Fold in half and insert in an open square to match stripe and knot fringe. Wrap end around fringe knot.

CUSHIONS

See photo on page 126

SIZE

Approx. 14" x 15¾".

MATERIALS

150 g white crochet cotton thread, 10 g each of the following colors: yellow, blue, green and pink. Steel crochet hook U.S. size 2. (U.K. size 2/0) For stripes: Crochet hook U.S. size E/4 and H/8. (U.K. size 9 and 6)

STITCHES USED

U.S. - Chain stitch (ch), single crochet (sc), double crochet (dc). U.K. - Chain stitch, double crochet, treble crochet.

GAUGE

16 squares in height and 14 squares in width = 4" x 4" using U.S. size 2 hook.

DIRECTIONS

Each cushion is made of 2 filet pieces. Ch 129 + ch 4 to turn (serves as first open square).
ROW 1: 1 dc in the 7th ch from the hook, *ch 1, skip 1 ch, 1 dc*, rep * to * across = 64 open squares.
ROW 2: Ch 4, 1 dc in the foll dc, *ch 1,

KEY TO CHART
□ = Open square
• = Filled square

Teacosy

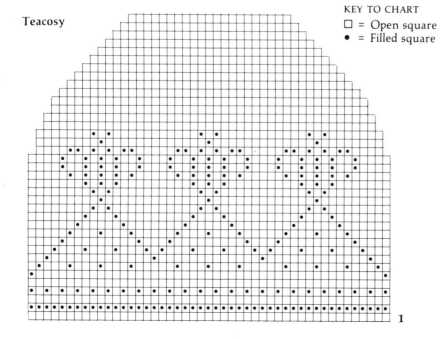

1

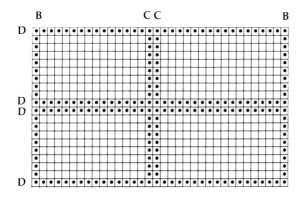

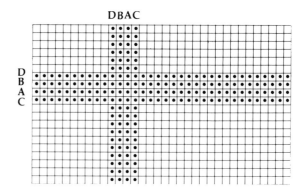

Color Charts for Cushions, page 126.

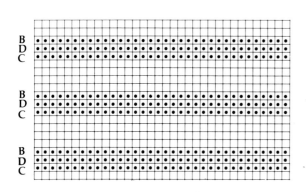

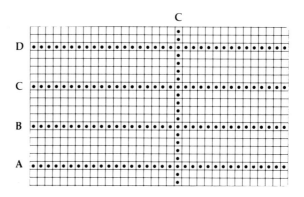

skip 1 st, 1 dc in the foll dc*, rep * to * across. Always rep row 2 until 40 rows are worked. Fasten off. Make a 2nd piece.

FINISHING

Pin piece to indicated measurement. Dampen and let dry. Stripes: with size H/8 hook work vertical stripes and size E/4 hook work horizontal stripes as on tablecloth. Fasten off the beg and end strand of each stripe. Follow the desired chart for stripe motif. Join the top and lower edges of pieces with 1 row of sc through both thicknesses. Along the side edges, work 2 sc in each open square, working 3 sc in the corners. Insert covered pillow form before closing the last side.

KEY TO CHARTS
A = Green
B = Yellow
C = Pink
D = Blue

TABLE RUNNER
See photo on page 128

SIZE
24¾" x 64½".

MATERIALS
400 g crochet cotton thread. Steel crochet hook U.S. size 7. (U.K. size 2½)

STITCHES USED
U.S. - Chain stitch (ch), slip stitch (sl st), double crochet (dc), triple crochet (tr). U.K. - Chain stitch, slip stitch, treble crochet, double treble crochet.

GAUGE
16 squares x 16 rows = 4" x 4".

Chart 1

KEY TO CHART
☐ = Open square
• = Filled square

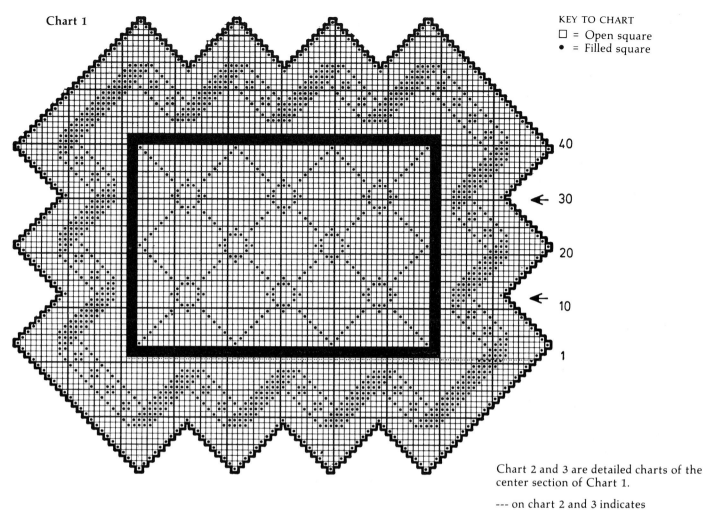

40

← 30

20

← 10

1

Chart 2 and 3 are detailed charts of the center section of Chart 1.

--- on chart 2 and 3 indicates continuation of pat

Chart 2

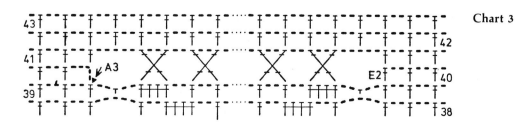

KEY TO CHARTS
▬ = Ch
†† = Dc
▲ = Sl st
‡ = Tr

Chart 3

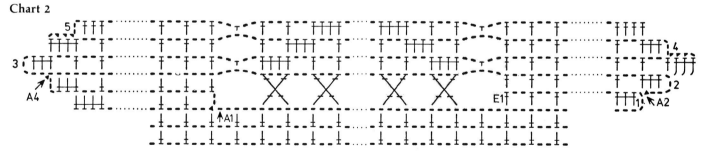

139

FILET CROCHET

Follow the charts. An open square = 1 dc, ch 2, skip 2 sts of previous row, 1 dc. A filled square = 4 dc. On the chart, the last st of 1 square serves as the first st of the foll square.

DIRECTIONS

Ch 234 + ch 3 to turn.
ROW 1: 1 dc in the 4th ch from the hook, 1 dc in each of the foll 2 ch, *ch 2, skip 2, 1 dc*, work * to * 5 times total, 1 dc in each of the foll 15 ch, work * to * 8 times total. Leave rem ch st unworked. Break yarn and join at right edge of row 1. Work row 2 of chart to heavy black line. Then ch 5 and work cross-stitch row across as shown on chart 2 (1 cross st and space: skip 8 ch, 1 tr in the 9th ch, ch 2, 1 tr worked in the 3rd ch st before the previous tr = cross st, *ch 2, skip 5 ch from the first tr of previous cross st, ch 2, 1 tr worked in 3rd ch st before previous tr*, rep * to * across). (Light dots on chart indicate continuation of pat.) Work to end of row, then ch 71 at left edge. In the 4th ch from the hook, work 1 dc. Work rows 3 to 11 on chart 1. The heavy black vertical line on chart 1 indicates the chain arcs shown on chart 2 (ch 5 to begin odd rows, ch 2 to begin even rows, 1 sc under the arc, ch 2 = ch arc). Rep the chart between the arrows 11 times, then work rows 30 to 39 of chart 1. Beg row 40, ending at point E2 on chart 3. Cut the yarn and rejoin at point A3. Work by foll chart, forming cross sts. When cross st row 6 is complete, resume work on chart 1. Complete chart 1, working each point separately. Fasten off. For the lower points, rejoin the yarn at point A4 on chart 2 (turn entire piece of work so that point A4 is at right edge of work). Work the row that begins at A4 to ch arc, then ch 2, sl st to join at corner of open work. Work back across row just completed. Complete lower edge by foll chart 1, working each point separately. Fasten off.

FINISHING

Pin piece to indicated measurement. Dampen and let dry.

TABLECLOTH

See photo on page 102

SIZE

Each square approx. 11" x 11".
Tablecloth approx. 33½" x 33½".

MATERIALS

350 g crochet cotton thread. Steel crochet hook U.S. size 6. (U.K. size 2)

STITCHES USED

U.S. - Chain stitch (ch), slip stitch (sl st), double crochet (dc). U.K. - Chain stitch, slip stitch, treble crochet.

GAUGE

16 squares in height and width = 4" x 4".

FILET CROCHET

Follow the chart.

DIRECTIONS

Ch 12 and sl st to join in a ring.
ROUND 1: Ch 3 (serves as first dc), 3 dc, *ch 5, 4 dc in ring*, rep * to * 3 times, ch 5, sl st to join round to the 3rd ch of the turning ch. Continue by foll chart from rounds 2 to 21 (chart shows ¼ of square. Work other ¾ of square to correspond). Fasten off. Make 9 squares. Join squares into 3 rows of 3 squares by sewing tog with fine stitches. Work 1 row of dc all around outside edges of tablecloth working 5 dc in each corner. Sl st to join. Fasten off.

FINISHING

Pin piece to indicated measurement. Dampen and let dry.

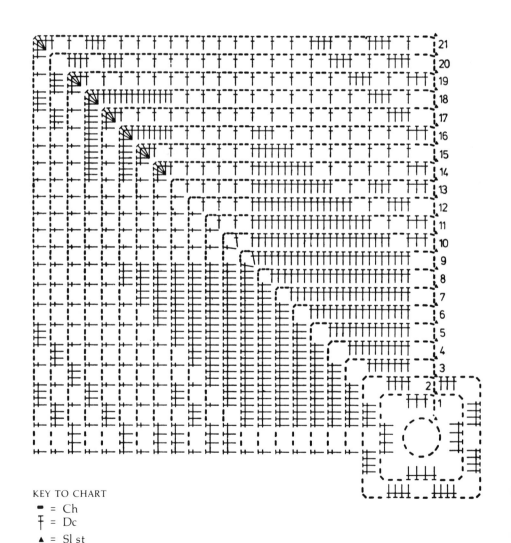

KEY TO CHART

- = Ch
⊤ = Dc
▲ = Sl st

INSTRUCTIONS FOR PANELS AND DOILIES

Continued from page 24

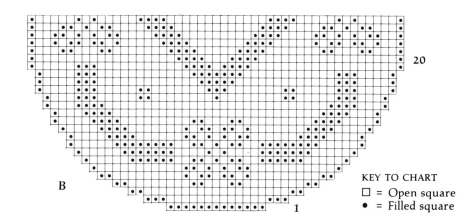

B

KEY TO CHART
□ = Open square
• = Filled square

20

1

DOILY

See photo on page 18 B

SIZE

Approx. diameter of 8½".

MATERIALS

20 g crochet cotton thread. Steel crochet hook U.S. size 10. (U.K. size 4)

STITCHES USED

U.S. - Chain stitch (ch), double crochet (dc). U.K. - Chain stitch, treble crochet.

GAUGE

21 squares x 23 rows = 4" x 4".

FILET CROCHET

Follow the chart. An open square = 1 dc, ch 2, skip 2 sts of previous row, 1 dc. A filled square = 4 dc. On the chart, the last st of 1 square serves as the first st of the foll square.

DIRECTIONS

Ch 39 + ch 3 to turn (serves as first dc). ROW 1: 1 dc in the 4th ch from the hook, then work 1 dc in each ch across row = 40 dc. Continue by foll chart from rows 2 to 25, then work rows 24 to 1. Work inc and dec by foll chart. Beg each even row with ch 3 and always work the last dc in the 3rd ch of the turning ch of previous row. Fasten off.

FINISHING

Pin pieces to indicated measurement. Dampen and let dry.

DOILY

See photo on page 18 C

SIZE

Approx. 12½" x 10½".

MATERIALS

30 g crochet cotton thread. Steel crochet hook U.S. size 10. (U.K. size 4)

STITCHES USED

U.S. - Chain stitch (ch), double crochet (dc). U.K. - Chain stitch, treble crochet.

GAUGE

21 squares x 23 rows = 4" x 4".

FILET CROCHET

Follow the chart. An open square = 1 dc,

ch 2, skip 2 sts of previous row, 1 dc. A filled square = 4 dc. On the chart, the last st of 1 square serves as the first st of the foll square.

DIRECTIONS

Ch 209.
ROW 1: 1 dc in the 8th ch from the hook, (= 1 open square), then continue by foll

chart = 68 squares. Continue by foll chart from rows 2 to 62. Beg each row with ch 3 and always work the last dc in the 3rd ch of the turning ch of previous row. Fasten off.

FINISHING

Pin pieces to indicated measurement. Dampen and let dry.

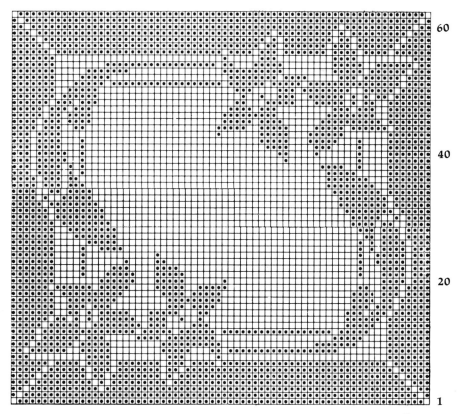

60

40

20

1

KEY TO CHART
□ = Open square
• = Filled square

C

141

DOILY

See photo on page 18 D

SIZE

Approx. 6" x 11¾".

MATERIALS

20 g crochet cotton thread. Steel crochet hook U.S. size 10. (U.K. size 4)

STITCHES USED

U.S. - Chain stitch (ch), double crochet (dc). U.K. - Chain stitch, treble crochet.

GAUGE

21 squares x 23 rows = 4" x 4".

FILET CROCHET

Follow the chart. An open square = 1 dc, ch 2, skip 2 sts of previous row, 1 dc. A filled square = 4 dc. On the chart, the last st of 1 square serves as the first st of the foll square.

DIRECTIONS

Ch 99 + ch 3 to turn (serves as first dc). ROW 1: 1 dc in the 4th ch from the hook and in each foll ch = 100 dc. Continue by foll chart from rows 2 to 69. Beg each row with ch 3 and always work the last dc in the 3rd ch of the turning ch of previous row. Fasten off.

FINISHING

Pin pieces to indicated measurement. Dampen and let dry.

D

KEY TO CHART

□ = Open square
● = Filled square

DOILY

See photo on page 18 E

SIZE

Approx. 10¼" x 11".

MATERIALS

20 g crochet cotton thread. Steel crochet hook U.S. size 10. (U.K. size 4)

STITCHES USED

U.S. - Chain stitch (ch), double crochet (dc). U.K. - Chain stitch, treble crochet.

GAUGE

21 squares x 23 rows = 4" x 4".

FILET CROCHET

Follow the chart. An open square = 1 dc, ch 2, skip 2 sts of previous row, 1 dc. A filled square = 4 dc. On the chart, the

KEY TO CHART

□ = Open square
● = Filled square

DOILY

See photo on page 18 F

SIZE

Approx. 12½" x 8½".

MATERIALS

20 g crochet cotton thread. Steel crochet hook U.S. size 10. (U.K. size 4)

STITCHES USED

U.S. - Chain stitch (ch), double crochet (dc). U.K. - Chain stitch, treble crochet.

GAUGE

21 squares x 23 rows = 4" x 4".

FILET CROCHET

Follow the chart. An open square = 1 dc, ch 2, skip 2 sts of previous row, 1 dc. A filled square = 4 dc. On the chart, the last st of 1 square serves as the first st of the foll square.

DIRECTIONS

Ch 39 + ch 3 to turn (serves as first dc). ROW 1: 1 dc in the 4th ch from the hook, then work 1 dc in each ch across row = 40 dc. Continue by foll chart from rows 2 to 33, then work rows 32 to 1. Work inc and dec by foll chart. Begin each even row with ch 3 and always work the last dc in the 3rd ch of the turning ch of previous row. Fasten off.

FINISHING

Pin piece to indicated measurement. Dampen and let dry.

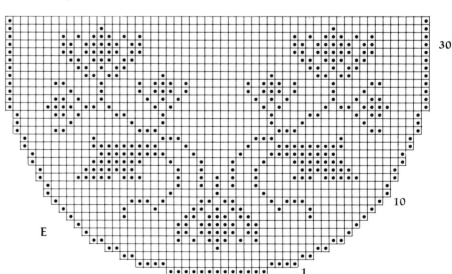

E

DIRECTIONS

Ch 201 + ch 3 to turn (serves as first dc).

ROW 1: 1 dc in the 4th ch from the hook and in each foll ch = 202 dc. Continue by foll chart from rows 2 to 26, then work row 25 to row 1. Beg each row with ch 3 and always work the last dc in the 3rd ch of the turning ch of previous row. Fasten off.

FINISHING

Pin piece to indicated measurement. Dampen and let dry.

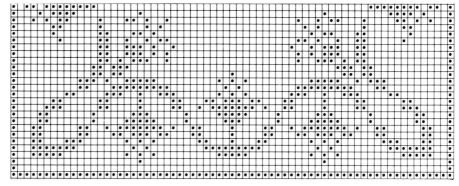

CLOWN WALLHANGING

See photo on page 20 A

SIZE

Approx. 10¼" x 10½".

MATERIALS

30 g crochet cotton thread. Steel crochet hook U.S. size 12. (U.K. size 5) 43¼" long wire 1/10" in diameter.

KEY TO CHART

□ = Open square   • = Filled square

STITCHES USED

U.S. - Chain stitch (ch), single crochet (sc), double crochet (dc). U.K. - Chain stitch, double crochet, treble crochet.

GAUGE

24½ squares in height and width = 4" x 4".

FILET CROCHET

Follow the chart. An open square = 1 dc, ch 1, skip 1 st of previous row, 1 dc. A filled square = 3 dc. On the chart, the last st of 1 square serves as the first st of the foll square.

DIRECTIONS

Ch 124 + ch 3 to turn (serves as first dc).

ROW 1: 1 dc in the 4th ch from the hook, 1 dc in each of the foll ch = 125 dc. Continue by foll chart from rows 2 to 66. Beg each row with ch 3 and always work the last dc in the 3rd ch of the turning ch of previous row. Fasten off.

FINISHING

Pin piece to indicated measurement. Dampen and let dry. Bend the wire to the same shape as the wall hanging and tape the ends together. Whipstitch edges around wire or join to wire by working 1 row of sc around wire. Fasten off.

HOUSE WALLHANGING

See photo on page 20 B

SIZE

Approx. 10¼ x 10¾".

MATERIALS

30 g crochet cotton thread. Steel crochet hook U.S. size 12. (U.K. size 5) 43¼" long wire 1/10" in diameter.

STITCHES USED

U.S. - Chain stitch (ch), single crochet (sc), double crochet (dc). U.K. - Chain stitch, double crochet, treble crochet.

GAUGE

24½ squares in height and width = 4" x 4".

FILET CROCHET

Follow the chart. An open square = 1 dc, ch 1, skip 1 st of previous row, 1 dc. A

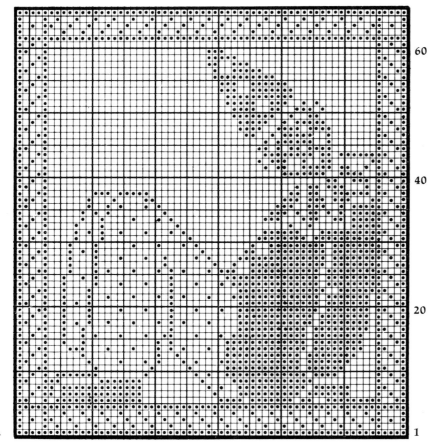

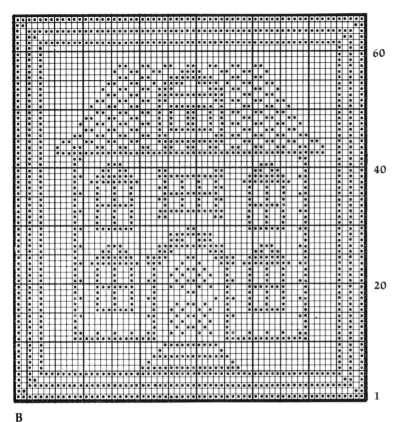

B

100

80

60

40

20

1

C

60

40

20

1

filled square = 3 dc. On the chart, the last st of 1 square serves as the first st of the foll square.

DIRECTIONS

Ch 124 + ch 3 to turn (serves as first dc).
ROW 1: 1 dc in the 4th ch from the hook, 1 dc in each of the foll ch = 125 dc. Continue by foll chart from rows 2 to 66. Beg each row with ch 3 and always work the last dc in the 3rd ch of the turning ch of previous row. Fasten off.

FINISHING

Pin piece to indicated measurement. Dampen and let dry. Bend the wire to the same shape as the wall hanging and tape the ends together. Whipstitch edges around wire or join to wire by working 1 row of sc around wire. Fasten off.

RIDER WALLHANGING
See photo on page 20 C

SIZE
Approx. 7½" x 16½".

MATERIALS
40 g crochet cotton thread. Steel crochet

KEY TO CHARTS

☐ = Open square
● = Filled square

hook U.S. size 12. (U.K. size 5) 49¼" long wire 1/10" in diameter.

STITCHES USED

U.S. - Chain stitch (ch), single crochet (sc), double crochet (dc). U.K. - Chain stitch, double crochet, treble crochet.

GAUGE
24½ squares in height and width = 4" x 4".

FILET CROCHET
Follow the chart. An open square = 1 dc, ch 1, skip 1 st of previous row, 1 dc. A filled square = 3 dc. On the chart, the last st of 1 square serves as the first st of the foll square.

DIRECTIONS

Ch 92 + ch 3 to turn (serves as first dc).
ROW 1: 1 dc in the 4th ch from the hook, 1 dc in each of the foll ch = 93 dc. Continue by foll chart from rows 2 to 100. Beg each row with ch 3 and always work the last dc in the 3rd ch of the turning ch of previous row. Fasten off.

FINISHING

Pin piece to indicated measurement. Dampen and let dry. Bend the wire to the same shape as the wall hanging and tape the ends together. Whipstitch edges around wire or join to wire by working 1 row of sc around wire. Fasten off.

Instructions continued on page 157

PILLOWS AND ACCESSORIES

Pillows and accessories are a quick and wonderful way to add the beauty of filet crochet to your home or the homes of special friends and relatives.

Below, an edging of filet crochet with a traditional snowflake motif attaches simply to an ordinary pillow. (see page 152 for directions) The gathered corners give the pillow an elegant look, reminiscent of Victorian styling.

PILLOWS AND ACCESSORIES

Right, *the designer of this colorful array of filet crochet pillows used the shapes of the pieces from many children's and adult's board games as inspiration for the geometric motifs. (see page 152 for directions) Using colored crochet thread instead of traditional white gives the pillows a bright, sporty look.*

C

E

F

PILLOWS AND ACCESSORIES

Nestled in a white wicker linen chest, the filet crochet pillows **shown here** would make a beautiful accent to any room of your home (see page 155 for directions) One pillow uses a large center rose with a floral border, while the other pillow features a wreath of roses.

Pattern graphs from other projects in this book, such as a tablecloth or a bedspread, can often be used to make a pillow or other accessory.

PILLOWS AND ACCESSORIES

S mall filet crochet panels can also be used to make unique tote bags. **Left**, crochet thread in colors of the rainbow forms a bright tote bag that uses a strip of fabric as its bottom. (see page 156 for directions) **Right**, any small motif designs in this book can be used on a tote bag. Or you can trace the outline of a favorite object, such as the tennis ball **shown here**, (see page 156 for directions) and use a gridded sheet of paper to make your own graph.

D on't limit your design planning to the filet projects in this book. Other accessory ideas include:

- sachet bags
- small jewelry bags
- tiebacks for curtains
- napkin rings
- x-mas ornaments
- antimacassars

INSTRUCTIONS FOR PILLOWS AND ACCESSORIES

PILLOW BORDER

See photo on page 145

SIZE

Pillow approx. 13″ x 13″. Approx. width of border 3¼″. Each pat repeat is approx. 2¾″. Pillow form 12″ x 12″.

MATERIALS

40 g crochet cotton thread. Steel crochet hook U.S. size 10. (U.K. size 4) Batiste fabric 15¾″ x 35½″.

STITCHES USED

U.S. - Chain stitch (ch), double crochet (dc). U.K. - Chain stitch, treble crochet.

GAUGE

22 squares x 23 rows = 4″ x 4″.

FILET CROCHET

Follow the chart. An open square = 1 dc, ch 2, skip 2 sts of previous row, 1 dc. A filled square = 4 dc. On the chart, the last st of 1 square serves as the first st of the foll square.

DIRECTIONS

Ch 42 + ch 3 to turn (serves as first dc).
ROUND 1: 1 dc in the 4th ch from the hook, 1 dc in each of the foll ch = 43 dc. Continue by foll chart from rows 2 to

16, then work rows 17 to 32, 24 times, end with rows 33 to 49. Beg each row with ch 3 and always work the last dc in the 3rd ch of the turning ch of previous row. Work inc and dec as shown on chart. Fasten off.

FINISHING

Pin piece to indicated measurement (65¼″ x 3¼″). Dampen and let dry. Cut fabric 13″ x 13″, allowing for ¾″ seam allowance. Sew last row of border to first row of border. With right sides together, sew 3 sides. Turn right side out, insert pillow form. Tack pillow to center. Sew 4th side. Sew all around pillow form. See photo. Sew on border around pillow, overlapping edge by ¾″. Place 4 motifs on each side and 2 motifs at each corner, gathering at corners to fit. See photo.

PILLOW COVER

See photo on page 146 A

SIZE

Approx. 14½″ x 14½″.

MATERIALS

100 g pink crochet cotton thread. Steel crochet hook U.S. size 6 (U.K. size 2). Black fabric 17¾″ x 39¼″. Stuffing.

STITCHES USED

U.S. - Chain stitch (ch), double crochet (dc). U.K. - Chain stitch, treble crochet.

GAUGE

12.5 squares in height and width = 4″ x 4″.

FILET CROCHET

Follow the chart. An open square = 1 dc, ch 2, skip 2 sts of previous row, 1 dc. A filled square = 4 dc. On the chart, the last st of 1 square serves as the first st of the foll square.

DIRECTIONS

Ch 138 + ch 3 to turn (serves as first dc).
ROW 1: 1 dc in the 4th ch from the hook, 1 dc in each of the ch sts = 139 dc. Continue by foll chart from rows 2 to 46. Beg each row with ch 3 and always work the last dc in the 3rd ch of the turning ch of previous row. Fasten off.

FINISHING

Pin piece to indicated measurements. Dampen and let dry. Cut fabric to 14½″ x 14½″ with ¼″ seam allowance. With

right sides tog, sew 3 sides tog. Insert stuffing and sew last side closed. Sew on crocheted piece to front.

See chart A on page 153

PILLOW COVER

See photo on page 146 B

SIZE

Approx. 15¼″ x 15¼″.

MATERIALS

100 g turquoise crochet cotton thread. Steel crochet hook U.S. size 6 (U.K. size 2). Black fabric 17¾″ x 39¼″. Stuffing.

STITCHES USED

U.S. - Chain stitch (ch), double crochet (dc). U.K. - Chain stitch, treble crochet.

GAUGE

12.5 squares in height and width = 4″ x 4″.

FILET CROCHET

Follow the chart. An open square = 1 dc, ch 2, skip 2 sts of previous row, 1 dc. A filled square = 4 dc. On the chart, the last st of 1 square serves as the first st of the foll square.

DIRECTIONS

Ch 144 + ch 3 to turn (serves as first dc).
ROW 1: 1 dc in the 4th ch from the hook, 1 dc in each of the ch sts = 145 dc. Continue by foll chart from rows 2 to 48. Beg each row with ch 3 and always work the last dc in the 3rd ch of the turning ch of previous row. Fasten off.

FINISHING

Pin piece to indicated measurements. Dampen and let dry. Cut fabric to 15¼″ x 15¼″ with ¼″ seam allowance. With right sides tog, sew 3 sides tog. Insert stuffing and sew last side closed. Sew on crocheted piece to front.

See chart B on page 153

Both American and British stitches are listed under STITCHES USED in each pattern, however, only the American terms are used in the text. British readers should convert these instructions to British terms as they work the projects.

KEY TO CHART

□ = Open square
• = Filled square

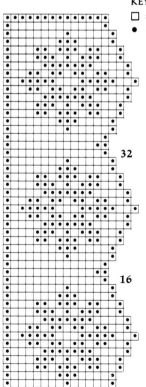

32

16

1

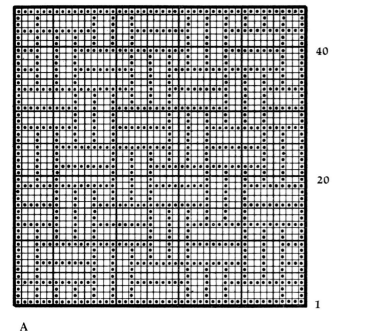

A

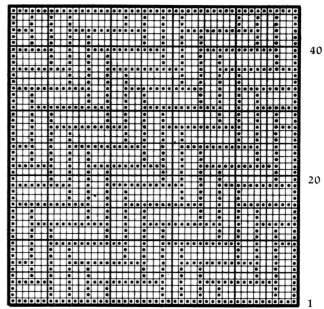

B

KEY TO CHARTS
□ = Open square
● = Filled square

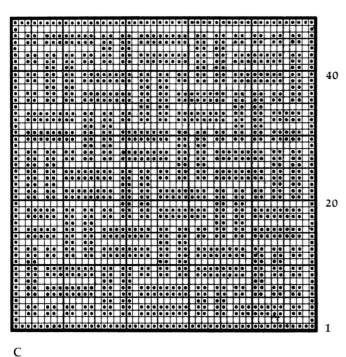

C

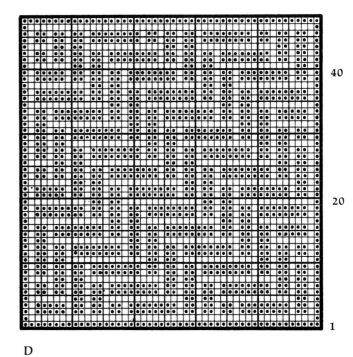

D

PILLOW COVER
See photo on page 146 C

SIZE
Approx. 15¼″ x 15¼″.

MATERIALS
100 g apricot crochet cotton thread.
Steel crochet hook U.S. size 6 (U.K. size
2). Black fabric 17¾″ x 39¼″. Stuffing.

STITCHES USED
U.S. - Chain stitch (ch), double crochet
(dc). U.K. - Chain stitch, treble crochet.

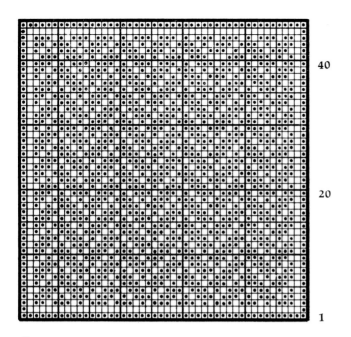

40

20

E

1

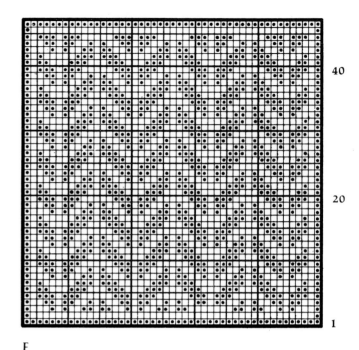

40

20

F

1

GAUGE

12.5 squares in height and width
= 4" x 4".

FILET CROCHET

Follow the chart. An open square = 1 dc,
ch 2, skip 2 sts of previous row, 1 dc. A
filled square = 4 dc. On the chart, the
last st of 1 square serves as the first st
of the foll square.

DIRECTIONS

Ch 144 + ch 3 to turn (serves as first
dc).
ROW 1: 1 dc in the 4th ch from the hook,
1 dc in each of the ch sts = 145 dc.
Continue by foll chart from rows 2 to
48. Beg each row with ch 3 and always
work the last dc in the 3rd ch of the
turning ch of previous row. Fasten off.

FINISHING

Pin piece to indicated measurements.
Dampen and let dry. Cut fabric to 15¼"
x 15¼" with ¼" seam allowance. With
right sides tog, sew 3 sides tog. Insert
stuffing and sew last side closed. Sew on
crocheted piece to front.

See chart C on page 153

PILLOW COVER

See photo on page 146 D

SIZE

Approx. 14½" x 14½".

MATERIALS

100 g green crochet cotton thread. Steel

crochet hook U.S. size 6 (U.K. size 2).
Black fabric 17¾" x 39¼". Stuffing.

STITCHES USED

U.S. - Chain stitch (ch), double crochet
(dc). U.K. - Chain stitch, treble crochet.

GAUGE

12.5 squares in height and width
= 4" x 4".

FILET CROCHET

Follow the chart. An open square = 1 dc,
ch 2, skip 2 sts of previous row. A
filled square = 4 dc. On the chart, the
last st of 1 square serves as the first st
of the foll square.

DIRECTIONS

Ch 138 + ch 3 to turn (serves as first
dc).
ROW 1: 1 dc in the 4th ch from the hook,
1 dc in each of the ch sts = 139 dc.
Continue by foll chart from rows 2 to
46. Beg each row with ch 3 and always
work the last dc in the 3rd ch of the
turning ch of previous row. Fasten off.

FINISHING

Pin piece to indicated measurements.
Dampen and let dry. Cut fabric to 14½"
x 14½" with ¼" seam allowance. With
right sides tog, sew 3 sides tog. Insert
stuffing and sew last side closed. Sew on
crocheted piece to front.

See chart D on page 153

PILLOW COVER

See photo on page 147 E

SIZE

Approx. 14½" x 14½".

MATERIALS

100 g light blue crochet cotton thread.
Steel crochet hook U.S. size 6 (U.K. size
2). Black fabric 17¾" x 39¼". Stuffing.

STITCHES USED

U.S. - Chain stitch (ch), double crochet
(dc). U.K. - Chain stitch, treble crochet.

GAUGE

12.5 squares in height and width
= 4" x 4".

FILET CROCHET

Follow the chart. An open square = 1 dc,
ch 2, skip 2 sts of previous row. A
filled square = 4 dc. On the chart, the
last st of 1 square serves as the first st
of the foll square.

DIRECTIONS

Ch 138 + ch 3 to turn (serves as first
dc).
ROW 1: 1 dc in the 4th ch from the hook,
1 dc in each of the ch sts = 139 dc.
Continue by foll chart from rows 2 to
46. Beg each row with ch 3 and always
work the last dc in the 3rd ch of the
turning ch of previous row. Fasten off.

FINISHING

Pin piece to indicated measurements.
Dampen and let dry. Cut fabric to 14½"
x 14½" with ¼" seam allowance. With
right sides tog, sew 3 sides tog. Insert
stuffing and sew last side closed. Sew on
crocheted piece to front.

PILLOW COVER

See photo on page 147 F

SIZE

Approx. 14¾" x 14¾".

MATERIALS

100 g yellow crochet cotton thread.
Steel crochet hook U.S. size 6 (U.K. size
2). Black fabric 17¾" x 39¼". Stuffing.

STITCHES USED

U.S. - Chain stitch (ch), double crochet
(dc). U.K. - Chain stitch, treble crochet.

GAUGE

12.5 squares in height and width
= 4" x 4".

FILET CROCHET

Follow the chart. An open square = 1 dc,
ch 2, skip 2 sts of previous row, 1 dc. A
filled square = 4 dc. On the chart, the
last st of 1 square serves as the first st
of the foll square.

DIRECTIONS

Ch 141 + ch 3 to turn (serves as first
dc).
ROW 1: 1 dc in the 4th ch from the hook,
1 dc in each of the ch sts = 142 dc.
Continue by foll chart from rows 2 to
47. Beg each row with ch 3 and always
work the last dc in the 3rd ch of the
turning ch of previous row. Fasten off.

FINISHING

Pin piece to indicated measurements.
Dampen and let dry. Cut fabric to 14¾"
x 14¾" with ¼" seam allowance. With
right sides tog, sew 3 sides tog. Insert
stuffing and sew last side closed. Sew on
crocheted piece to front.

See chart F on page 154

ROSE PILLOW COVERS

See photo on page 148

SIZE

15¾" square.

MATERIALS

110 g crochet cotton thread. Steel
crochet hook U.S. size 7. (U.K. size 2½)
A covered pillow sized to match covers.

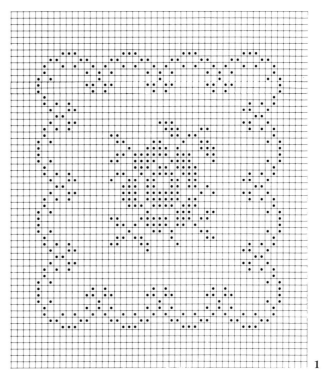

Chart 1

KEY TO CHARTS

☐ = Open square
● = Filled square

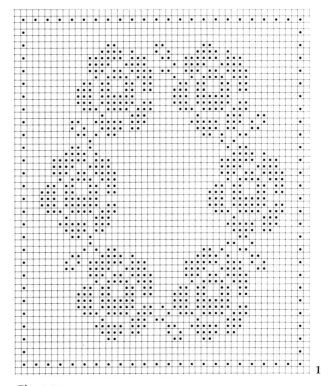

Chart 2

155

STITCHES USED

U.S. - Chain stitch (ch), single crochet (sc), double crochet (dc). U.K. - Chain stitch, double crochet, treble crochet.

GAUGE

12 squares x 14 rows = 4" x 4".

FILET CROCHET

Follow the chart. An open square = 1 dc, ch 2, skip 2 sts of previous row, 1, 1 dc. A filled square = 4 dc. On the chart, the last st of 1 square serves as the first st of the foll square.

DIRECTIONS

Ch 148 + ch 5 to turn (serves as first open square).
ROW 1: 1 dc in the 9th ch from the hook, *ch 2, skip 2 ch, 1 dc in the foll ch*, work * to * across = 49 open squares. Continue by foll chart 1 or 2. At the end of every row, turn and ch 5 for the first open square. Fasten off. Make a 2nd piece.

FINISHING

Pin piece to indicated measurement. Dampen and let dry. With wrong sides tog, work 1 row of sc around edges, working through 2 thicknesses. Work 2 sc in each open square and 4 sc in each corner square. Join 3 sides, slip in pillow and crochet closed the last side. Fasten off.

BEACH BAG PURSE

See photo on page 150

SIZE

Approx. size of crochet piece 18" x 25¼".

MATERIALS

20 g crochet cotton thread in each of the foll colors: yellow, orange, red, pink, purple, dark blue, turquose and green. Piece of yellow cotton fabric 9¾" x 19¾". Piece of yellow vinyl about 9¼" in diameter. Steel crochet hook U.S. size 2. (U.K. size 2/0)

STITCHES USED

U.S. - Chain stitch (ch), double crochet (dc). U.K. - Chain stitch, treble crochet.

GAUGE

11 squares in height and 10½ squares in width = 4" x 4".

DIRECTIONS

With gold, ch 211 + ch 5 to turn (serves as first open square). Work back and forth.

ROW 1: 1 dc in the 9th ch from the hook, *ch 2, skip 2, 1 dc in the foll ch*, rep * to * across = 70 open squares.
ROW 2: Ch 5, 1 dc in next dc, *ch 2, 1 dc in the dc of the previous row*, rep * to *. Rep row 2 as foll: 4 rows of gold, 6 rows of orange, 6 rows of red, 6 rows of pink, 6 rows of purple, 6 rows of dark blue, 6 rows of turquoise and 6 rows of green. Fasten off.

FINISHING

Pin piece to indicated measurement. Dampen and let dry. Sew piece lengthwise, using matching color thread. Fold the yellow fabric in half and cut a circle with an 8¼" diameter + ¼" seam allowance. With right sides tog, sew around edges of circle, leaving an opening to turn. Turn right side out. Cut a piece of yellow vinyl with an 8" diameter and insert inside yellow fabric circle. Sew opening closed. Sew to lower edge of crocheted piece. Make a cord (using all colors tog) about 55" long and thread through holes at upper edge. See photo.

GREEN BEACH BAG

See photo on page 151

SIZE

Approx. 10¼" x 15¾".

MATERIALS

125 g green crochet cotton thread. Steel crochet hook U.S. size 11. (U.K. size 4½)

STITCHES USED

U.S. - Chain stitch (ch), slip stitch (sl st), double crochet (dc). U.K. - Chain stitch, slip stitch, treble crochet.

GAUGE

10 squares in height and width = 4" x 4".

FILET CROCHET

Follow the chart. An open square = 1 dc, ch 2, skip 2 sts of previous row, 1 dc. A filled square = 4 dc. On the chart, the last st of 1 square serves as the first st of the foll square.

DIRECTIONS

BOTTOM

Ch 5 and sl st to join.
ROUND 1: Ch 3, *ch 2, 1 dc in ring*, work * to * 5 times, end with ch 2 and sl st to join. Continue by foll bottom chart. When bottom chart is complete, work filet chart around bottom piece.
ROUND 1: Ch 5, *skip 2 dc, 1 dc in the foll ch, ch 2*, rep * to * around, sl st to the 3rd ch of turning ch to join in round.
ROUND 2: Ch 5 to turn, *skip 2, 1 dc in the foll dc, ch 2*, rep * to * to end of round, end with 1 dc in the foll dc, ch 2, sl st to the 3rd ch of turning ch to join in round. Continue by foll chart until piece measures 15¾". Beg each round with ch 5 and always sl st to 3rd ch of the turning ch of previous row. Fasten off.

FINISHING

Make a cord and thread through top round of filet section.

KEY TO CHART

□ = Open square
● = Filled square

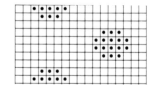

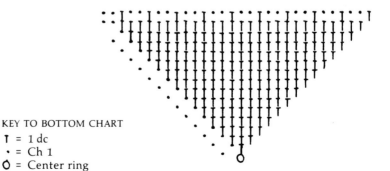

KEY TO BOTTOM CHART

T = 1 dc
· = Ch 1
○ = Center ring

⅙ of Bottom Chart

156

Continued from page 144

CAT WALLHANGING

See photo on page 20 D

SIZE

Approx. 9½ x 11½".

MATERIALS

30 g crochet cotton thread. Steel crochet hook U.S. size 12. (U.K. size 5) 43¼" long wire 1/10" in diameter.

STITCHES USED

U.S. - Chain stitch (ch), single crochet (sc), double crochet (dc). U.K. - Chain stitch, double crochet, treble crochet.

GAUGE

24½ squares in height and width = 4" x 4".

FILET CROCHET

Follow the chart. An open square = 1 dc, ch 1, skip 1 st of previous row, 1 dc. A filled square = 3 dc. On the chart, the last st of 1 square serves as the first st of the foll square.

DIRECTIONS

Ch 116 + ch 3 to turn (serves as first dc).
ROW 1: 1 dc in the 4th ch from the hook, 1 dc in each of the foll ch = 117 dc. Continue by foll chart from rows 2 to 70. Beg each row with ch 3 and always work the last dc in the 3rd ch of the turning ch of previous row. Fasten off.

FINISHING

Pin piece to indicated measurement. Dampen and let dry. Bend the wire to the same shape as the wall hanging and tape the ends together. Whipstitch edges around wire or join to wire by working 1 row of sc around wire. Fasten off.

VASE WALLHANGING

See photo on page 20 E

SIZE

Approx. 10½" in diameter.

MATERIALS

30 g crochet cotton thread. Steel crochet hook U.S. size 12. (U.K. size 5) 35½" long wire 1/10" in diameter.

STITCHES USED

U.S. - Chain stitch (ch), single crochet (sc), double crochet (dc). U.K. - Chain stitch, double crochet, treble crochet.

D ... 70 / 50 / 30 / 10 / 1

KEY TO CHART
□ = Open square
● = Filled square

GAUGE

24½ squares in height and width = 4" x 4".

FILET CROCHET

Follow the chart. An open square = 1 dc, ch 1, skip 1 st of previous row, 1 dc. A filled square = 3 dc. On the chart, the last st of 1 square serves as the first st of the foll square.

DIRECTIONS

Ch 36 + ch 3 to turn (serves as first dc).
ROW 1: 1 dc in the 4th ch from the hook, 1 dc in each of the foll ch = 37 dc. Continue by foll chart from rows 2 to 64. Work inc and dec by foll chart. Beg each row without incs or decs with ch 3 and work the last dc in the 3rd ch of the turning ch of previous row. Fasten off.

FINISHING

Pin piece to indicated measurement. Dampen and let dry. Bend the wire to the same shape as the wall hanging and tape the ends together. Whipstitch edges around wire or join to wire by working 1 row of sc around wire. Fasten off.

See chart E on page 159

ROOSTER WALLHANGING

See photo on page 20 F

SIZE

Approx. 10¼" x 10¼".

MATERIALS

30 g crochet cotton thread. Steel crochet hook U.S. size 12. (U.K. size 5) 37½" long wire 1/10" in diameter.

STITCHES USED

U.S. - Chain stitch (ch), single crochet

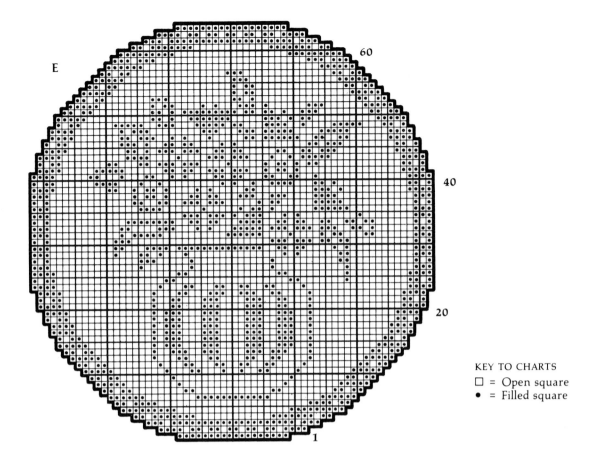

E

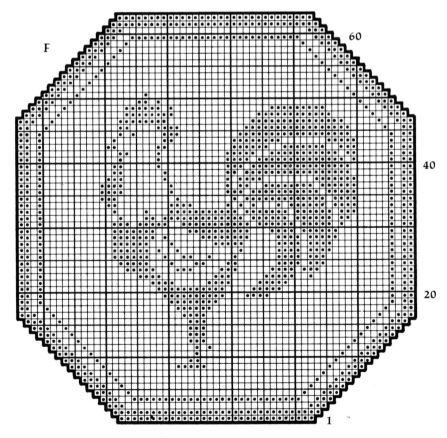

F

KEY TO CHARTS
□ = Open square
• = Filled square

(sc), double crochet (dc). U.K. - Chain
stitch, double crochet, treble crochet.

GAUGE
24½ squares in height and width
= 4" x 4".

FILET CROCHET
Follow the chart. An open square = 1 dc,
ch 1, skip 1 st of previous row, 1 dc. A
filled square = 3 dc. On the chart, the
last st of 1 square serves as the first st
of the foll square.

DIRECTIONS
Ch 62 + ch 3 to turn (serves as first dc).
ROW 1: 1 dc in the 4th ch from the hook,
1 dc in each of the foll ch = 63 dc.
Continue by foll chart from rows 2 to
63. Work inc and dec by foll chart. Beg
each row without incs or decs with ch 3
and work the last dc in the 3rd ch of the
turning ch of previous row. Fasten off.

FINISHING
Pin piece to indicated measurement.
Dampen and let dry. Bend the wire to
the same shape as the wall hanging and
tape the ends together. Whipstitch
edges around wire or join to wire
by working 1 row of sc around wire.
Fasten off.

158

INDEX